BEYOND THE CHURCHES

BEYOND THE CHURCHES

Edited by Peter Brierley

Facing a Task Unfinished:
Groups outside the churches
in England and Wales

MARC EUROPE

EVANGELICAL ALLIANCE

Address for Evangelical Alliance
Whitefield House
186 Kennington Park Road
London SE11 4BT
(01-582 0228)

Address for MARC Europe
146 Queen Victoria Street
London EC4V 4BX
(01-248 3056)

BV
3777
.E5
B48
1984

British Library Cataloguing in Publication Data

Beyond the churches
  1. Evangelistic work — England
  I. Brierley, Peter
  269'.2'0942   BV3777.G7

  ISBN 0-9508396-8-X

The Evangelical Alliance brings together Bible-believing Christians to be a united voice to the nation and an encouraging and initiating force in the churches. The ministry of Evangelical Alliance is exercised through the departments of prayer and revival, churches, evangelism, and government and media.

MARC Europe is an integral part of World Vision, an international Christian humanitarian organisation. MARC's object is to assist Christian leaders with factual information, surveys, management skills, strategic planning and other tools for evangelism. We also publish and distribute related books on mission, church growth, management, spiritual maturity and other topics.

CONTENTS

ACKNOWLEDGEMENTS

I should like to express my thanks to Susan Harrison, Research Administrator at MARC Europe, for her oversight of this extensive piece of research; and to Alf Chown, who joined MARC to work on the collation of the mass of information which the survey produced. Their painstaking and committed efforts were essential for this project to come to fruition.

I should also like to thank Clive Calver and Patrick Johnstone for contributing hard-hitting and effective articles despite heavy schedules, and to acknowledge the massive debt which the Christian churches owe to Ed Dayton, vice-president of World Vision International and founder of MARC, who has been a pioneer thinker in the whole area of people groups.

Peter Brierley
August 1984

INTRODUCTION

Peter Brierley
*European Director,
MARC Europe*

How it began

One part of the jigsaw fell into place on a visit to see Patrick Johnstone, the International Research Secretary at WEC International's headquarters at Bulstrode, near Gerrards Cross.

'How many adults in England and Wales do you reckon never go to church?' he asked.

'About 35 million, judging from the church survey reports *Prospects for the Eighties* and *Prospects for Wales*.'

'That's a very large number. They must break down into smaller groups.'

'What groups would you suggest?' I asked.

'Well, there are probably at least three types. There are the various ethnic groups, often with their own language and culture — Italians as well as West Indians. Then there are various community groups, each touching on different parts of English society.'

'Can you give examples?'

'Steel workers, or the folk in a local old people's home. Some of these will have members who are Christians, but some will not. There is a third type also, rather more elusive, of people who come together for a temporary reason, such as when they travel together, or are working on a particular project.'

'Not the sort that you would build a church for?'

'No, but they do present an opportunity for evangelism, with those who become Christian integrated into existing churches.'

Another part of the jigsaw came in a conversation with Clive Calver, the enthusiastic General Secretary of the Evangelical Alliance. He was very keen on the idea of a survey.

'You mean an exercise whereby some of the many folk who don't go to church now might be identified a little more precisely?'

'Yes.'

'That fits precisely into our hopes for next year's Leadership Conference and our strategy beyond. It could help the churches see something of the opportunities in their neighbourhood.'

A third piece of the jigsaw came from those who were freshly introduced to the *Unreached Peoples* Directories annually published by MARC International since 1979. 'It would be good if there was a similar study, more detailed, but related only to this country,' they said.

Tom Houston, then Executive Director of the Bible Society, was asked his opinion on such a study. 'Do it if you can,' he said. 'The timing seems right, as 1984 is the year of Mission England and Mission to London. It is important to think through what happens next.'

The jigsaw became complete as a small number of folk in different denominations were approached. All were supportive, and we have been most grateful for all the help given by this temporary Council of Reference. They are:

Rt Rev. Michael Whinney, Bishop of Ashton
Rev. Jeffrey Harris, Home Mission Division, Methodist Church
Rev. Lewis Misselbrook, Adviser in Evangelism, Department of Mission, Baptist Union
Mr Michael Eastman, Secretary and Development Officer, Frontier Youth Trust
Rev. Patrick Johnstone, International Research Secretary, WEC International
Mrs Vincie Thomson, Evangelism Secretary, Evangelical Alliance
Mr Peter Searle, Director, World Vision of Britain.

They have given their advice both on the broad concept of the survey and the actual questionnaires used.

What were we trying to do?

We wanted to produce a resource tool to stimulate evangelistic strategies, endeavour and concern for the millions of non-Christians in our land. They are men and women, young, middle-aged, single or in families, who are not in touch with a local church. They may live in the inner city, outer suburbs or rural areas. They may be rich or poor, with a good job, part-time or unemployed. They may be black or white. They may be British or Indian, Asian or European. They may be single or married. They may live in a semi-detached, a council house, or on a caravan site. The one thing they have in common is that they are not linked with a Christian church regularly.

Methodology

We decided to seek information on three groups of folk outside the churches. This information would be representative and in no way exhaustive or comprehensive. Groups mentioned in one county might well exist in other counties or towns, but would not be cross-referenced. The groups chosen were:

(1) *Ethnic/linguistic groups* who will often be immigrants, frequently speaking as their mother tongue a language other than English. They may have been in this country for many years or just a few months. In many cases there will not be a local church in which they will naturally feel at home, whose culture and customs reflect their home background. They may be Chinese, Pakistanis, West Indians or refugees. They may be shop-keepers, bus drivers, or managers.

(2) *Social/Community groups* who will frequently be British men and women who see the Church as irrelevant to their needs, even if there is a church in their locality with which they could be linked if they so wished. They will mainly be grouped either by geography — living in the same set of flats, for example — or by workplace: the same offices or factory. They may well define themselves in terms of class, a vital factor in planning evangelism in the UK. A key feature of these groups is that while a church would not be formed specifically for one such group, a church could well be planted or re-oriented to serve several groups in the locality.

(3) *Occasional groups* may be a mixture of the first two groups whose activities or situation may be described as constituting essentially an opportunity for outreach. *Normally no congregation would be formed specially for these groups.* They may be suburban commuters, housewives at a pre-school children's play group, youngsters keen on their motorbikes, members of a prestigious local club, or senior citizens at a regular get-together.

A random selection was made of nearly 6,400 church leaders, over 6,000 of whom were clergymen. The sample included people from all denominations and churches. Each was sent an explanatory letter, details of the study, and three questionnaires, one for each of the groups identified above.

The questions asked for a brief description of the group, what tied the group together, its location, and whether the folk lived in any special part of the town or suburbs, and for how long. How many were in the group? Did the group include men and women? Were there any Christians in the group? If so, roughly what percentage? What denominations had most contact with the group? Were there churches of these or other denominations in the locality? Was anyone undertaking any Christian outreach amongst them? What types of need would the majority in the group be conscious of? What might be the main blocks to their knowing and experiencing the Good News of Jesus Christ?

Additional questions were included on the 'ethnic groups' form, about their mother tongue, the religion of the majority, their country of origin, and roughly what percentage might be able to read English easily. The occasional groups form also asked about the regularity with which the group came together, whether this group presented any special kind of opportunity for Christian outreach or service, and what approach might be particularly suitable for members of this group.

A total of 637 completed forms were received, a response rate of just over 10%. Whilst this is very low by normal survey standards, the number of forms sent out was deliberately chosen to give a return of about 600 forms (the rate of return having been estimated from a pilot study). 600 forms were judged to give a reasonable representation across the various counties and groups and yet be contained in a Report whose published price would still hopefully ensure a good distribution. 59% of the forms returned described Social/Community groups; 27% Occasional groups; and 14% Ethnic/Linguistic groups. The survey is essentially qualitative and descriptive of particular groups. In addition a further 200 or so replies were received from ministers unable to complete a form but willing to give some information or positive response. This broad methodology can always be reconsidered for any subsequent similar study.

Statistics

The two Reports mentioned earlier (*Prospects for the Eighties,* and *Prospects for Wales*) give information on the number of people who attend church by county. Their age and sex is also given. These numbers were projected forward to 1984 assuming the same rate of change as occurred between 1975-1979 for English counties and 1978-1982 for Wales. The same approximate age and sex distribution was assumed. The numbers were subtracted from the latest census of population figures for each county, to give the total number of people who do not regularly attend church, broken down by age-group and sex. These figures were then rounded to the nearest thousand.

These numbers thus give an approximate idea of those still outside the Christian Church in every part of the country. Not all would consider themselves non-Christian or even non-religious. Some will be church members who, despite this, only attend services occasionally. Others will be those who attend at Christmas or Easter or at someone's marriage or christening. Others will have a religious faith but not a Christian one — they will be Buddhists, Hindus, Muslims or Sikhs. The large majority of these people will however be outside the churches in the sense of being strangers to the family of God who regularly worship Him with others. They need to know about and experience the Good News of Jesus Christ.

Where do we go from here?

Our hope is that this book should act as a stimulus to local evangelism. We hope church leaders and others will find this kind of description helpful and that it will enable them to plan more effective ways of reaching these and similar groups. We hope too that many other groups will be identified.

The majority of the groups described have some Christians among them. Most have churches in their area in touch with the people in the group. Yet more often than not the outreach being undertaken seems to be casual; something that happens from time to time but isn't part of a strategic plan. Many saw times of family celebration or grief as an opportunity for Church involvement. Others talked of the need for the Church to assume a community role running clubs for Mums and Toddlers, elderly folk or young people.

The Church's outreach seems to be perceived in terms of responding to people's social needs. When asked to describe the main blocks to the group knowing and experiencing the Good News of Jesus Christ, again the answers were often formulated in social terms. The group was either too wealthy, or too poor. They were described as being self-sufficient or independent and having no need for the Church. Over and over again the respondents said that the group saw the Church as irrelevant. It was not often that they talked of sin or Satanic intervention keeping people from God.

As we plan our evangelism, there are clearly social questions to be asked. Why is the Church seen as socially irrelevant? But if we are to plan evangelism, then we must have our aim in mind. *This survey would seem to indicate that there are key questions to be asked not only about why people are not being reached, but more importantly, why is it that we want to reach them anyway?*

As far as is known, this is the first time a study of this kind has been undertaken in this country. Any comments on it will be most welcome. It is certain that many groups will not have been included, and if the reader would like to give us details of some of these, they will be gratefully received. If reactions to this study are generally positive, it may well be repeated.

What is MARC Europe?
MARC Europe is a ministry of World Vision, a Christian organisation specialising in relief, development, child sponsorship and church leadership training. MARC acts as a strategy unit within World Vision, conducts large scale religious research projects, undertakes a seminar programme to apply these results to local situations, and consultancy work for churches and Christian organisations. This study was funded by MARC Europe as a service to the churches in England and Wales.

BEYOND OUR GHETTOS!
SUGGESTIONS ON
HOW TO USE THIS SURVEY

Clive Calver
General Secretary,
Evangelical Alliance

1984 will be remembered.

With affection. With respect. In appreciation. The year of the big missions will not be forgotten. But the nature of our corporate memory could well prove to be the turning point for the spiritual life of our nation. The question is whether or not renewed spiritual activity will continue. If not, then we are condemned to an on-going development of comatose redundancy in our churches. A few thousand converts do not constitute revival; but they do demonstrate a startling potential for all that could happen if we regain God's agenda for his Church in the nation.

The danger is that we could well conclude that we now have an effective recipe for proclaiming the Christian message at all times.

(i) Invite an international evangelist.
(ii) Advertise him and listen to his message.
(iii) Integrate converts into the church and start all over again.

I find it very significant that few people I talk with on this matter appreciate the fact that consciously there is little debate. Only a handful would endorse the policy described. There is a tremendous groundswell of opinion demanding that the Church recognises the principles of an army of ordinary people compassionately sharing in the needs of a hurting society. An army which can then share the message of biblical truth, as the Gospel is gossiped up and down the length and breadth of this nation.

Many have appreciated the fact that there is little point arranging meetings, or demonstrating in the open air, to proclaim the fact that 'Jesus is the answer' when in fact nobody is actually asking the question! A radical demonstration of evangelical concern in the community, for the individual and between Christians themselves is the first prerequisite if we are then to have authority in the message of biblical truth which we proclaim.

Along with these concerns has been needed a radical re-emphasis on the importance of Christian lifestyle — a return to the biblical priorities of prayer, of a stand on the solid ground of Scripture and a rediscovery that God has a role for all of us to play. Above all, a touch from God expressing that this nation is ready for a mighty outpouring of the Spirit of God through an army of ordinary people. A torrent of Spirit-anointed sermons, articles and books are reiterating these same principles.

It is not the purpose of this manual to go over that ground which has been covered far more eloquently elsewhere. But it is our purpose to ask why this reawakened concern for evangelism and evangelical confidence has not yet materialised into those solid gains which provide the foundation on which we may build. One could quote many instances of church congregations who have transformed theories of evangelism into a vital demonstration of community involvement and spiritual power as they serve their Lord within their own geographic locality. Yet the fact remains that by and large we have not even begun to scratch the surface of spiritual ignorance and apathy among ordinary people within this nation.

Priority of the task

The commands and instruction from Jesus were quite straightforward. 'I have been given all authority in heaven and on earth. Go, then, to all peoples everywhere and make them my disciples' (Matt. 28 vv. 18-19).

Peter asserted, 'Be ready at all times to answer anyone who asks you to explain the hope you have in you' (1 Pet. 3 v. 15). And Paul was instructed by the Holy Spirit to continue the emphasis in the words, 'If you confess that Jesus is Lord and believe that God raised him from death, you will be saved. For it is by our faith that we are put right with God; it is by our confession that we are saved' (Rom. 10 vv. 9-10).

Even the Psalmist joined the consensus of opinion. 'Let the redeemed of the Lord say so' (Psa. 107 v. 2, AV), he enjoined them, and those words retain their eternal authority on us and on our lives. The crucial imperative to confess our faith is gloriously applicable to all of us today. We are not commanded to struggle in order to work out what to say. Nor are we encouraged to develop pet formulae or specific methods. We are told to be available to the Holy Spirit, that he might give us the words, the life, the opportunity to bring glory to Jesus by confessing our love for Him.

It would be too easy for us to examine our own weaknesses or inadequacies in order to claim that God could never use us! The danger lies in our false humility blinding us to all that God has implanted in us and therefore all that God longs to achieve through our lives. A perfect Creator could never produce useless creatures and he does have a great and unique role for each and every one of us. Graham Kendrick has summarised it in these words:

'One shall tell another, and he shall tell his friend,
Husbands, wives and children shall come following on,

From house to house in families shall more be
gathered in,
And lights will shine in every street, so warm and
welcoming.'

I find it profoundly significant that when three of us
journeyed to Nice in order to invite Dr Graham to
come to Mission England, his condition of accep-
tance was that his meetings would be no more than a
focus for encouragement and hope by which local
churches might be stimulated into an on-going focus
on evangelism.

Problem of the age

There has long existed an apparent tension between
things of the mind and those of the spirit. Increasingly the pressure has come to expect the
miraculous and ignore the analytical instead of
recognising that within all the joys of the super-
natural explosion of the power of God, the early
church developed their own strategy and maintained
their own statistics.

'Many wonders and miraculous signs were done
by the apostles. All the believers were together
and had everything in common. Selling their
possessions and goods, they gave to anyone as
he had need. Every day, they continued to meet
together in the temple courts. They broke bread
in their homes and ate together with glad and
sincere hearts, praising God and enjoying the
favour of all the people. And the Lord added to
their number daily those who were being saved'
(Acts 2 vv. 43-47).

Before we can properly diagnose a solution to the
needs of our age, we must first adequately clarify the
problem. We live in a nation where — whether we like
to accept it or not — nearly ninety per cent of the
people have not heard who Jesus is, or what he can
achieve in their lives! In other words, we are not living
in a nation which is full of people actively rejecting
the claims of Jesus in their lives, but one where most
people have no genuine concept of who he really is.

The myth of Britain as a Christian nation must be
exploded in a new awareness of the true state of
affairs.

(1) This is a pluralistic nation. I live in a city which
has no cathedral apart from a Buddhist temple
where Christian clergy and Buddhist monks
worship together!
(2) This is a Satanically invaded realm. London has
been called by an enterprising group of travel
agents 'the occult capital of the world'. Throughout all strata of society there is demonstrated a
rabid interest in occultism in all its forms.
(3) This country confronts a watershed of spiritual
ignorance. Faced with an unholy alliance of
doubting clergy and sceptical media interests, it
is little wonder that genuine understanding of
Christianity has declined. Friends of mine have
enquired in the classroom 'what is a Christian?',
and been greeted by the reply 'someone who
drinks tea!' It has even been suggested that the
answer could be 'someone born in England', or
'someone who grows their own vegetables!' In

fact, one girl went into a jewellers to purchase a
pendant; she rather liked a cross and looked at a
crucifix in bewilderment. 'Who is the man on it?'
she asked!
(4) This is a class-ridden nation, and the Christian
faith has become a middle-class religion. It is
seen in practice as irrelevant to the working man.
We need to free our faith from its cultural
entrapment.

Province of our message

In the face of these disturbing facts, the time has
come to address ourselves to reality rather than to
the world as we would like it to be. In the cold light of
day it has become apparent to thinking evangelicals
that our whole understanding of the nature and
character of evangelism requires a radical overhaul
in three specific areas. It is into these very areas that
the research and content of this book has been
addressed.

(1) Evangelism must become less cyclical and more
statistical in its approach. After thirteen years in
full-time evangelism I have become totally
convinced of the need to develop a strategic
understanding of the task of the Church as
God's divinely appointed agent in evangelism
today. His instruction to us was to be the gospel
to all people. Their response is a matter between
the human heart of the individual and the
sovereign will of the Father God. The nature of
our task is to convey the message, clearly and
coherently through our lives, prayer, words and
actions. No more and no less!

For too long evangelism has been perceived
as a series of missions conducted every one,
two or three years by professional evangelists
who come to serve us in evangelism with the
regularity of the seasons themselves. Tragically
the style and performance is often stereotyped
by tradition and little impact is made on society
as a whole.

Now this is not designed as a broadside
against my fellow-evangelists but as a protest
against the patterns of thought to which we
either restrict ourselves, or are constricted by
the churches we are seeking to serve.

Instead of this cyclical and repetitive
approach being accepted as the inevitable
pattern, we should perhaps ask three questions
about it.
(a) Are large numbers of unchurched people being
drawn into intelligent enquiry about Christianity,
or are our meetings full of the faithful?
(b) Do we measure success by the numbers
challenged by the Christian message, or by the
percentage who were left totally unreached by
the whole initiative? There is a big difference
between saying one hundred non-Christians
heard the content of the Gospel and faced up to
its implications and saying that 99.3 per cent of
the unchurched population were never aware of
what was going on.
(c) Are we exposing people to Christian truth who
have already heard and rejected that message?

In other words they are culturally drawn to the Church but have become 'Gospel-hardened'. Or are we addressing our message to those for whom it has all the impact of something that is a relatively new, fresh and exciting challenge? Now these could easily be misunderstood as harsh words which blindly ignore all that God is doing through established means, methods and missions. That is never my intention. I rejoice along with the apostle Paul at all means that are employed by the Holy Spirit to bring people into a genuine repentance and commitment to Christ. My questions are aimed at provoking urgent enquiry to God as to whether we are fulfilling his mandate and priority for evangelism in our area. In other words, they are aimed at asking whether or not we are truly getting people from hell to heaven or whether we are only going through the comfortable, familiar motions of doing evangelism as a duty in the manner to which we have become accustomed. Our intentions are good but so much more could be achieved!

(2) Evangelism must be less oriented around the professional evangelists and more around the potential of the people.

Don't get me wrong! God is calling more people today into the ministry of evangelism than for many years. That ministry is great. It is valid and used of God. But not all are called into it full-time.

Church growth experts assure us of two things: first, ten per cent of the average church population are directly gifted in evangelism; second, all the rest of us have ministries in witness, prayer, and lifestyle to communicate the love of Jesus Christ to our neighbours, friends and community.

In other words, we have a vast workforce within the church which is largely unused. The reason is that many of us would gladly get more involved if only we could recognise how, and to whom!

(3) Evangelism must be more concentrated on those who have never heard for primarily cultural reasons. It may be utterly abhorrent for us to admit it but our place in society is a vital factor as to whether or not we become aware of the content of the Christian message.

This is, of course, a generalisation and as such does not allow for sovereign outreach from God which transcends sociological barriers. But that apart, the working-class/single parent/un-employed/ inner city/ northerner is far less likely to hear the message than the middle-class/ family man/ civil servant/ suburban/southerner! Such factors must never become acceptable to us. Paul admitted that he was 'compelled to preach. Woe to me if I do not preach the Gospel' and commented, 'I make myself a slave to everyone to win as many as possible . . . I have become all things to all men so that by all possible means I might save some' (1 Cor. 9 vv.

16, 19, 22, NIV). His aim must be ours . . . 'I have fully preached the Gospel of Christ, thus making it my ambition to preach the gospel not where Christ has already been named, lest I build on another man's foundation but as it is written, "They shall see who have never been told of him and they shall understand who have never heard of him" ' (Rom. 15 vv. 19-21).

Since the majority of unreached people in our nation are working class, and the church is not, then the inevitable implication is that we will have to face up to hard questions. How do we plant new congregations, creating an effective evangelical witness where none exists? How do we become more down-market? Are we pre-pared to move house to a less favourable area, as one friend of mine recently did? Dare we accept lower positions in terms of employment or social station in order to reach people for Jesus? Hard issues, but requiring radical answers. Determining to discover God's agenda for our lives, we should reject the intrusive demands of our social grouping in order to face up to the priorities which the love of Jesus lays on us as his servants.

We need to become more conscious of those in our own areas who are unreached with the Christian message. Having identified such people we can then do something about it!

Purpose of our mission

This survey was commissioned as the fulfilment of a dream. It was designed to encourage us all in seven specific areas that we might face the challenges of our day. Not by dictating our responsibilities, but in fulfilling Christ's charge to us as his people that we might go into the highways and byways to bring people to the King.

(i) Stimulating leadership: it is hoped that the illus-trations will encourage leaders to recognise the need to leave no-one in our generation unchurched or unreached.

(ii) Identifying opportunity: why not use the survey as an illustration and conduct your own analysis of specific groups in your locality — and start to reach them.

(iii) Adopt an unchurched group: in your house-groups, youth work, church or fellowship, adopt a local unchurched group and one mentioned in the survey. Establish contact for prayer and offer help and support where it is needed. For example, if your church is in Bromley and the unchurched group you adopt from elsewhere is in Ramsbottom, use your resources to en-courage Christians there to meet the needs!

(iv) Use the statistics: to wake up the sleepers among us to face the needs of those who are suf-fering spiritual starvation within our nation. While I worked as part of the ministry of British Youth for Christ, we often utilised a picture of people walking to work across London Bridge, and beneath it we placed the caption 'Help the starv-ing millions'. Shock tactics are required to wake us up. Use the statistics as a tool in that way.

As Jesus himself reminded us, 'As long as it is day, we must do the work of him who sent me. Night is coming, when no-one can work' (John 9 v. 4, NIV).

(v) Determine a strategy by collecting information and mobilising the church or fellowship to prayerfully fulfil the mandate to reach a specific unreached group.

(vi) Use the material for specific prayer. Pass out one group in the survey for each church family to pray for. Let members individually adopt such groups for real penetrating prayer. TEAR Fund have used this strategy effectively to tackle specific areas of need overseas; let's use it here too.

(vii) Develop creative means to meet local needs. Drop-in centres for the unemployed, care groups for unmarried mums, etc., etc. Let's learn from illustrations of how God is using his people to combat need elsewhere by being prepared to use similar means in our own area to face up to human need and present the love and claims of Jesus Christ to those who have never heard his message of life!

In less organised fashion within a simpler society, our spiritual forefathers faced the challenge of their own generation. Horseback preachers, parliamentary reformers, trades union pioneers, teachers, welfare workers, nurses, social activists — all stood as lights to the world. Their aim was to reach the unreached and draw them into the family of the Church. Their impact touched the heart of our eighteenth and early nineteenth century nation. It is estimated that half of Britain heard the Gospel — and God can and will do it again. But are we prepared for it to be through us?

This survey gives us the nature of the problem. It is for us before God to determine whether or not we are prepared to let him make us to be part of his answer for a dying land.

THAT EVERYONE MAY HEAR:
THE CONCEPT OF PEOPLE GROUPS

Ed Dayton
Vice-President for Mission and Evangelism,
World Vision International

*This article is adapted from parts of **That Everyone May Hear** (MARC, 1983) by Ed Dayton, and **Planning Strategies for World Evangelisation** (Eerdmans, 1980) by Ed Dayton and David Fraser. Both volumes are available in the UK from MARC Europe.*

There are now more than four and a half billion people in the world; almost one-third call themselves Christians. That includes all Protestants, Catholics and Orthodox. But more than three billion others do not follow Christ. If we divided up the world's population between those who call themselves Christians and those who do not, the picture would look something like this:

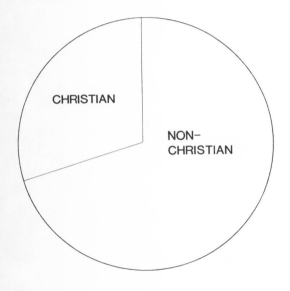

Although the number of Christians is growing, so is the overall population of the world. The ratio of Christians to non-Christians has remained more or less constant for the past fifty years.

If we narrow the focus to England and Wales, however, since that is the scope of the survey recorded in this book, then the picture is not even as encouraging as the static situation described above. Reliable figures for attendance for all churches are not available for decades gone by, but *membership* rolls have been falling for many years now. Recent attendance patterns are a little more encouraging, but it is clear that the task facing Christians in England and Wales is daunting.

Only 9% of the adults in England, and 13% of the adults in Wales, actually attend church on the average Sunday. Or, to put it the other way, 91% of the adults in England and 87% of the adults in Wales do *not* attend church. This follows the general picture to be found in the whole of Western Europe — a post-Christian, materialistic, secular society in which the churches all too frequently huddle together and look inwards, becoming progressively less relevant and losing what vision they have of winning the world for Christ. In their increasing isolation they fail to realise that Western Europe is the only significant part of the world, with the exception of Africa north of the Sahara, where Christianity is not actually on the increase.

The situation in Western Europe is grim, from a Christian viewpoint. Yet to abandon ourselves to cynicism and holy huddles is to ignore both the sovereign power of God and the mandate we have received from our Lord Jesus. He has commanded his Church to make disciples of all nations, including our own. Every Christian in every local church, in every country of the world, is called upon to be a witness to the saving power of Christ.

If we claim Jesus as Lord, God's command to us is that we should proclaim our faith by what we say and how we live. This is in fact what is happening. On every continent, often with startling effect, men and women are gossiping the Gospel to their friends, their neighbours, to the village or city in which they live. By spontaneous sharing and by organised witness the Good News is going forth.

In addition to these local witnesses God has set apart certain men and women to go out and reach those groups and those towns and cities where as yet there is no local proclamation of the Gospel. But the task cannot be left to them alone, despite the feeling in many parts of the Western Church that religion is the clergy's business.

In England and Wales the resources are there. Even 9% of adults in England can be translated into four million people. That is not an inconsiderable number. If each adult Christian told three other people about Christ each year for three years, then the task would be done! This is certainly part of the work of the local church. Some of those told would be 'nominal' Christians. Some would be adherents of other faiths. More would have no faith at all, and would consider themselves agnostics or atheists.

In practice, however, it is simply unrealistic to think in such broad terms. For one thing, many Christians will just not have a contact of any strength with that many non-Christians. For another, there is often a substantial class barrier between Christians and non-Christians in Britain: membership of the churches tends to come from the upper socio-economic groups. They will not use the same idiom, or have the same presuppositions or world-view as those they are trying to reach. Thirdly, it is a foolish error to lump all non-Christians together; different people and different areas have vastly differing needs and openness to the Gospel.

How do you evangelise the world?
World evangelisation is the major task of the Church. We need to see churches planted among the two billion people and more who do not know Christ, have not even heard of Christ. In England and Wales, that will mean reaching the 35 million adult people who are *beyond the churches.*

The job is awesome, too big to grasp. How can you in practice present the Gospel in an effective way to a nation, whether it is Britain or India or Finland? A nation simply varies too much. Different loyalties, different interests, different ambitions, different occupations and often different languages — all divide the whole into many parts. How can you present the Gospel to a religious grouping? Even the minority faiths in Britain are often too big to work with. How can you present the Gospel even to a single town, when any community of more than a few thousand can have so many diverse concerns and prejudices that to reach one part of a locality may be to alienate another — or where the diversity is so great that very different approaches must be used?

One way of approaching the task, which is demonstrated in this volume, is to evangelise *one people group at a time.*

A people group is a significantly large grouping of individuals who perceive themselves to have a common affinity for one another. This bond may develop because of shared language, religion, ethnicity, place of residence, occupation, class or situation, such as a common adversity. We do not include nationality, because for most purposes a nation is too big to be regarded as a unit, from the point of view of evangelism.

Let us look at that definition in more detail.

'Significantly large' means a group large enough to believe itself to be a group. It might be a few dozen, or a few hundred: exceptionally it might be numbered in millions.

A 'grouping of individuals' means that a people group will be composed of people who relate to one another in a particular situation. They may live in the same place, such as a local village; they may have the same occupation, such as the men and women on the whaling fleet off South Africa; they may be facing a common hazard, as with groups of refugees — from many different classes and occupations — who find themselves fleeing together from one country to another.

'Who perceive themselves' needs some further refining. People who speak the same language would obviously perceive themselves as having some common affinity. So might those from the same ethnic background. But people in the same situation, even though they may not relate closely to one another on a day-to-day basis, may yet perceive themselves as having something in common. This would be true for example of dwellers in high rise flats in East London. They would scarcely interact on a daily basis, but might discover a latent affinity for one another because of their shared situation. This could have real importance from the evangelistic perspective.

We can express this principle by a series of diagrams.

This block of figures represents the people among whom you live — your neighbours and friends, the folk who are all around you.

You share a *locality* with others. Do you, and they, consider this locality to be important to yourselves? If so, the group becomes more clearly defined.

Perhaps not all of you share a common *language,* or as importantly, a common *idiom.* So let us draw a 'boundary' which represents language or idiom.

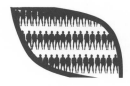

Do you live among different *ethnic* groups? Which is yours? Draw another boundary; the number of people we are discussing is further reduced.

Perhaps you are conscious of boundaries created by a class, or profession, or manner of dress. These are *social boundaries.*

Is the *religion* of your group important as part of the awareness of being a group? In Britain there is often a latent, unexpressed, but quite significant religious consciousness, often vaguely connected to the Church of England!

By this process we can begin to be aware of the many different people groups which make up our society. They overlap: frequently a single individual will be part of many different groups. Some groups will be transitory — a trainload of commuters on the Southern Region. Some will be vocational — union members, or teachers, or clerical staff in an office. Some will be social — members of a working men's club. Some will be defined primarily in terms of where they live: young mothers on a housing estate, for example.

The point of this exercise is to tailor an evangelistic approach to a specific group which will be particularly appropriate to that group. Just as every individual is unique, so every people group is unique. Each group requires, therefore, a unique strategy of evangelism. Indiscriminate evangelism will mean a great deal of wasted effort and all too often a dashing of hopes. Young Christians with a fire in their hearts to win men and women for Christ can find the harvest so meagre that they may grow discouraged. If we cast the seed forth indiscriminately then some is bound to fall on stony ground.

We need to discover God's approach, his best way of reaching a given group. Instead of searching for one grand strategy for the evangelism of Britain, we need to see that there is no one universal method. Each group deserves to hear the Gospel in a way that has been especially prepared by the Holy Spirit. It will require a unique group of evangelists, and a special combination of evangelistic approaches.

To talk in terms of reaching a nation for Christ is a wonderful vision. There is certainly a place for the big mission. But these need to be supplemented, at a level where we will not be overawed, by specific, local efforts to a specific, local group. When we recognise that God may be calling us to bring the Gospel to one particular group then the task becomes understandable and believable. Perhaps it is the group to which we ourselves belong. If someone is not asked to cross barriers of language or culture when he or she becomes a Christian, then the step of conversion is likely to be that much easier. Perhaps it is another group whom God has called to our attention. Sometimes we are called to a people far removed from our own.

The goal of this book is to demonstrate how you can become aware of viable people groups all around you. The survey on which the bulk of the text is based was undertaken to present examples of how this strategy can be used in the context of English and Welsh society.

Some advantages of a people-centred approach
At first sight this way of thinking may seem unduly structured and manipulative, owing more to pragmatic management techniques than to obedience to the Spirit of God. But this would be a false impression. 'People group thinking' has much to commend it.

It attempts to see the world as God sees it. The Lord of the universe is not only concerned with political boundaries, or with people as a whole, or simply with individuals, but also with the relationships which men have to one another.

It is a response to the Great Commission. The Lord tells us to go to all peoples. By a people-centred approach the Church may be mobilised.

It makes the task understandable. The scale of operation becomes more realistic and less awe-inspiring.

It defines a realisable goal. The churches of England and Wales are often discouraged by a hostile environment. General indifference, and the follow-my-leader cynicism of the media, sap the will to reach out with the Gospel message. But use elsewhere of the unreached peoples concept has shown that if 20% of a given group can be won to Christ, then the church so created is, under God, self-sustaining.

It defines the preparation needed. All too often evangelistic planning is woolly and idealistic. This approach can lead to a carefully thought out, specific strategy.

It helps communicate the task of mission. Churches tend to think of outreach only in terms of areas, but this approach allows much more precise and stimulating planning. This can be shared with church members far more vividly.

It changes the emphasis from sending to reaching. The Church is not in the business of sending missionaries, but of reaching peoples and making disciples.

It helps recruiting. When a task is well defined and comprehensible it is much more likely to stir the hearts of those whom God has chosen for that task.

It makes prayer support much stronger. 'Blanket' prayers are all too common, too sloppy and too short-lived. Persistent, thinking, informed prayer which expects answers is wholly biblical, and from experience, much more likely to see answers.

Understanding is the chief currency of successful evangelism
Christ cares about the hurts and aspirations of every person in every cultural group. As we begin to understand those hurts and aspirations, we can so fashion our presentation of the Gospel message that we create open channels of communication. But such understanding is not a currency that is easily earned.

Christ lived for many years among his chosen people before he started to teach. When he did begin his public ministry he spoke in the language of the people, and they flocked to hear him. He knew what was in the heart of man. By prayer, by the love that God gives us, by careful sharing and listening, we can follow the same path and speak with something of the same authority. We must follow the example of Christ.

There is no simple way of pulling back the veil. Charles Taber, in *Evangelizing the Unreached Peoples,* writes:

> The evangelist, before planning his approach, must discover what assumptions the hearer holds about reality, truth and value; and more important, must be keenly aware of what problems deeply trouble the hearer, so that he can maximise the fit of the Gospel presentation to the hearer's needs.

Three Key Areas
There are three key areas crucial to the understanding of a given people group: meanings, needs and behaviour (including institutions and relationships). By looking at these areas we can find several types of 'bridges' over which the Gospel can be conveyed. Each is crucial to successful evangelism.

Meanings
The first dimension deals with *what* people think and *how* they think. If the Gospel does not make sense

they will reject it. Everyone develops a system of meaning to make sense of the world and their experience of the world: what the universe is like, why they exist, what they can expect from life, how they can understand death, how they can communicate with others.

This system is made up of a number of different components.

(i) *Language* is a symbolic system of codes which assigns meaning to the world. But each language labels the world rather differently; and because the labels are different, even if only slightly, the worlds people live in will differ from group to group. As such language is fundamental to a group's identity. A first task then for an evangelist in Britain is to 'break the code', to get an adequate grasp of the local idiom so that he or she can enter the mind of the people.

(ii) *Hermeneutics* means the science of interpretation. How does a given people group think, how does it interpret the basic information received through language and experience? How do people formulate conclusions? How do they use 'intuition' or hunches or 'gut feelings'? Is intuition a more dominant method of interpretation than the logical syllogistic reasoning of the professional classes in the West? What counts as evidence? Is what is 'reasonable' simply a question of logical deduction? How do they test and accept new ideas?

(iii) *World View.* A world view is the governing set of concepts and presuppositions that a people lives by: a framework into which all other thoughts and concepts are placed. The language and hermeneutical systems of a people will reflect, express and reinforce the fundamental world view. This is crucial for evangelism: when for instance Paul was bitten by a snake the people of Melita concluded he was a god because he did not die. A western scientist would have reached a quite different, and possibly equally erroneous, conclusion. The rituals, preoccupations, superstitions and religious concepts of a given people group will give clues to their world view.

In presenting our message, we need to ask how much our target group knows about the Gospel, and how they react to what they know. Our message must be modified in its form to fit their world view and to build upon what understanding they do have. If we can understand the processes by which people come to faith then this will contribute substantially to our evangelism.

Needs
Evangelisation always takes place in the context of need. Christ not only expressed his teaching, masterfully, in the language and concepts of his audience, but he also ministered to their felt needs. He healed the blind, fed the hungry, forgave the guilty, accepted the outcasts. In doing so he broke a good number of social taboos. To each person he gave specific attention, meeting each at their point of individual need.

Jesus however did not deal only with subjectively felt needs. His own commitment to the Kingdom of God made him constantly aware of the objective discrepancy between what the world is and what his Father's Kingdom is. But Jesus did respond to felt needs, and used them to demonstrate the power and relevance of the Kingdom.

No culture is completely successful in meeting all the needs of its people. One of the results of sin is that any culture will have demonic as well as admirable qualities. It will throw up tensions, as people find it essential to live and cooperate with one another, but discover that intimacy gives rise to conflict. Beauty or intelligence or wealth are unevenly distributed, and the resulting resentments, tensions, anxieties and fears are some of the subjective drives which make up the daily existence of a given people group. As our society disintegrates, loneliness and boredom are the lot of both old and young.

Knowledge of these needs is essential for evangelism. People must feel the disruptive force of a need before they will be very open to the Gospel. Sometimes, of course, needs are not very conscious or 'felt'. Often there is an interaction between the person who brings the message of a new way of life and the person to whom the appeal is made. (A church offering fellowship can induce in the outsider an overwhelming sense of isolation.) A group may only feel dimly aware of something lacking or uncomfortable, and it is only when a presentation of the Gospel is made that the need is brought into sharper focus. Because of this it is often misleading to label a group as responsive or resistant: they may spurn one approach, but respond to another because it more clearly articulates the unspoken longing of that group.

How do we discover the felt needs of a people? Often the best way is simply to ask them! It is important to ask many people, not just two or three. We can cross-check by relating to later respondents what earlier respondents have said. More objective data are also indispensable. Superstition will often indicate a heavy emotional involvement, implying that a culture's technology cannot secure a desired end. In the UK, close adherence to superstitions may be shrugged aside, but the belief in the validity of superstitions is frequently a fundamental tenet even among those who scoff. More seriously perhaps, the widespread appeal of horoscopes indicates both a hunger for certainty and a hunger for significance in humdrum lives.

Another place to look for indications of need are in the ideals of a culture. Every person has some ideas about what an ideal adult lifestyle is like. Who has attained such ideals — be it a romantic marriage, or popularity, or the latest BMW? What are the things in a given culture or environment which prevent people from reaching such ideals for themselves?

The behaviour of Christians in local churches is also a clue! What are the common temptations to which they are subject? Do they vary with age, sex or status? Where the body of Christ is adequately meeting the needs of a people, temptation will decrease. (If gossip is rampant, what is that church teaching about fellowship and unity?) Where there are unmet needs, or a form of Christian faith that is not dynamically incarnated in a people's way of life, then alternative solutions to those needs will be found. By way of example, the Christian churches in Bantu Africa have provided healing services which relate well to the material and physical causes of illness — but witchdoctors still abound, for the churches have not provided an answer to such basic questions as to why people fall ill in the first place, or why one person experiences misfortune and not another. There are few witchdoctors in England and Wales, but virtually every newspaper and periodical carries a horoscope.

Guilt is also an indicator. Every society sets standards of right and wrong. There will be in many people groups in England and Wales a sense, latent but persistent, of guilt. This will certainly be experienced by the individual, but a group will often have a sense of obligation to particular goals or causes or people which is indicative of a more collective guilt. Collecting boxes for Oxfam will function as penances — unwelcome, yet cathartic — for the affluent societies of the South East. Need for forgiveness is objective. All stand before a just God as rebels who have sinned against his glory. This fundamental guilt is a felt need, often half-conscious. The Gospel can offer repentance and forgiveness.

Those who are lost, in their own eyes, are not always obvious. The dossers under Charing Cross Bridge think little of themselves. Their needs are plain to see, if not always so easy to remedy. But there are others all around us who wrestle with besetting sin, or a prevailing sense of uselessness or alienation, or a past or present crime. Frequently the simple failure to match the adverts is a crushing burden. Jealousy or hatred or insecurity or fear are all present, for all levels, in all groups. The Gospel can touch and heal.

Behaviour patterns
Behaviour patterns are the organised modes by which a people goes about meeting its needs in institutions, roles, social structures, and customs. Different customs and structures can act either as bridges or walls in the presentation of the Gospel. For a church to be established in a people group, it will have to relate its patterns of everyday living, worship and service to the common pattern already available.

From a theological viewpoint we must affirm the dignity and value of culture. Humanity, and human society, is a creation of God, and even in a fallen world much of our culture functions to hinder selfishness and to bring people together. Culture allows for the achievement of love and mutual concern.

Culture however is fallen. It can be evil. Selfishness exists in many institutional structures and customs. War, oppression, pride and racism are all to be found in such structures. The Christian Gospel will not only use cultural patterns and structures in proclaiming the Kingdom, but as with language and need it will re-define and judge. It thus exists in a tension with culture, present in that culture yet continually breaking out to find new 'wineskins' for its fresh new vision.

We cannot always predict which tensions will arise. Economic systems, justice, education and the

place of government of left or right, are all areas in which conflict with the Christian faith may occur. The outcome will not be clear and Christians often find themselves opposing one another. Yet the challenge of the Kingdom to the accepted order is an inescapable part of the proclamation of the Gospel message. A change of allegiance to Christ is a deep and radical event, and affects everything.

In presenting our faith, we will run up against the question: are there some cultural practices which are simply unacceptable to the Gospel? If we are to present the Gospel to the workers in an armaments factory, should Christ's message of peace be so interpreted that they would, if converted, be required to leave their jobs? Here the evangelist will need to be very aware of his own cultural baggage as he seeks to reach a particular group.

Three facets of behaviour
The culture of groups is often confusing. Three particular points may help to make the requirements for evangelism clearer.

(i) *Silent language.* A basic part of human communication is nonverbal behaviour. This will include physical characteristics of people, body language (gestures, motions, positions), spatial relationships, body contact and aesthetics. To get signals wrong in this field is to kill off real communication. Apart from the reinforcement of the verbal message by the non-verbal, one is quickly perceived as cold, uncaring or (most damning of all) simply strange. For this to be remedied, there is no substitute for spending a good deal of time with that group.

(ii) *Social structure.* People are organised into different social units by kinship, race, community or organisation, etc. A study of social structures will reveal the leaders and opinion formers in a group: if these are reached, even in our fragmented UK society, it is far more likely that people will be persuaded to truly hear the Gospel. Every politician knows this, which is why key journalists are so carefully treated. (Good relations with the local press should be encouraged by all churches!)

(iii) *Institutions.* Every society organises to solve its common problems. Over time it will develop formal and standardised patterns for handling various different affairs. A death will involve social services, health services, legal guidance, and religious ceremony. The individual does not have to devise a new pattern for each contingency but rather to learn and follow the pattern that exists.

A major part of understanding a people involves understanding its institutions. Knowing the expectations that go with being a host or a guest, a stranger or a friend, can open or close the relationship one is trying to create. These institutions are changing today: a generation ago it would have been customary to shake hands with a stranger, but for many young people, and for many blue-collar workers, a cautious nod of the head has usurped the handshake, which may now seem curiously stilted and overly formal, even arrogant. The guidelines grow daily more blurred.

If we are going to express our faith adequately to people groups in England and Wales, we are going to have to understand their meaning system (language, hermeneutics, world view); their needs and aspirations, and their social structure, institutions and silent language. By doing so we will make our message more culturally relevant. This will be cause for rejoicing: there is little that is more challenging or rewarding than to plant the seed that gradually grows into the body of Christ.

BRITAIN'S ETHNIC MINORITIES: A MISSION FIELD FOR LOCAL CHURCHES

Patrick Johnstone
International Research Secretary,
WEC International

Who ARE the British today?

Who would have dreamt 40 years ago that the British would be anything other than Anglo-Saxons, with a Celtic fringe to the north and west? Then we were reasonably clear about who an Englishman was! Large-scale immigration from all over the world and especially from the New Commonwealth has changed that. There are now brown, black and yellow as well as white people with British citizenship. Does one qualify by ethnic origin or by birth to be called an Englishman? So emotive is this discussion that it was impossible to ask an ethnic question in the 1981 census, so it is hard to obtain clear statistics on ethnic groups living in Britain today.

As Christians, we need to be aware of the present situation. Millions now live in Britain who come from lands that have had minimal exposure to the Gospel, and where the entry of missionaries is either forbidden or greatly restricted. We have an imported mission field of vital, strategic significance. Sadly very few local churches have seen this, or believe that they can do anything about it. Tragically, the greatest opportunity for evangelising the flood of new immigrants has passed. In the 50's and 60's they were more receptive to change. Let us not perpetuate this mistake, but bring the Gospel to them with love and sensitivity.

The size of Britain's ethnic minority population

At the time of the 1981 Census, 6% of our population was born outside Britain, i.e. 3,374,000 people. Many of these have married and had children that are British-born. This number may be around 2,000,000. So about 9% of our present population has foreign origins, and about half of this total are from New Commonwealth countries (in Asia, Africa and West Indies). In this group, only those of West Indian origin have a high proportion of committed Christians. Most of the others are Muslim (1,500,000), Hindu (500,000), Sikh (180,000), and Buddhist (120,000). Exposure to the Gospel in their lands of origin *and* in Britain has been minimal. This fact is abundantly borne out by the lists of unchurched ethnic/linguistic groups in this volume.

It is in some of our major cities that the ethnic variety is most visible. There are now over 1,000,000 belonging to ethnic minorities in London alone (14% of the total population), and in London schools there are children speaking 128 distinct languages in their homes! The percentages for Birmingham are 13%, Bradford 10%, Manchester 9%, etc. Our city congregations are the key for their evangelisation, yet what a sad reversal occurred several years ago when the Leicester Carey Memorial Church became the main Hindu temple of the city. William Carey was one of the great pioneer missionaries to India.

What brought these minorities here?

(1) *Immigration by work-seekers* from Southern Europe, and, since the war, a flood of citizens from the New Commonwealth. Over 500,000 of the latter entered Britain between 1955 and 1962, a flow that has now been much reduced by government legislation.

(2) *Flight — as Refugees* from Nazi German rule and conquest (Poles, Jews, etc.), Communist domination in Eastern Europe. More recently there have been the Vietnamese, Iranis and Afghans. Many have been assimilated to a greater or lesser extent, but pockets of real emotional and spiritual need are to be found among them all over the country. In 1982 there were 148,000 officially classified in this country as refugees.

(3) *Study* — in 1977 there were over 100,000 foreign students in our universities, polytechnics and language schools. The number has dropped slightly since then, but what a challenge! So many come from lands closed to missionary work, and have their first exposure to 'Christianity' here. They are frequently shocked by our post-Christian society, moral laxity and our unfriendliness. Yet it is among students in the West that some of the most significant conversions of Muslims to Christ have taken place.

(4) *Tourism* brings millions to our shores — many from the Muslim world. Do we milk them for their petro-dollars or give them the pure milk of the Word? Every plane-load or ship-load leaving Britain takes away hundreds of missed opportunities for sharing the Gospel.

(5) *Business and Diplomacy* — who ever even thinks of a ministry to the lonely Middle Eastern businessmen, financiers, and the isolated diplomats from such unevangelised lands as Mongolia, Maldives, Bhutan, and Libya?

From where do these ethnic minorities come?

The diagram on the next page shows the origin and numbers of ethnic minorities now residing in Britain. Together with our more indigenous non-Christian minorities they make up 15% of the population of the UK.

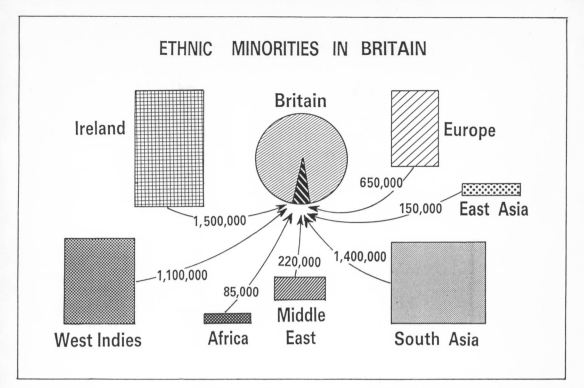

ETHNIC MINORITIES IN BRITAIN

Ireland 1,500,000

Britain

Europe 650,000

East Asia 150,000

West Indies 1,100,000

Africa 85,000

Middle East 220,000

South Asia 1,400,000

I have classified the ethnic minorities in eight major groups:

(1) *Minorities that have become indigenous over the centuries:*
(a) The 410,000 Jews. There has been a steady trickle of conversions to Christ, but the great majority remain unmoved by the Gospel. Note the seven entries on Jewish groups included in this volume.
(b) The 85,000 Gypsies. 30,000 of these are Romany speaking, and the rest are known as 'Irish Travellers' — few have ever come to an open commitment to Christ.

(2) *The Irish* — 612,000 born in the Republic live in the UK, but with unrestricted entry, and long residence, those of Irish descent may number three times this. There are stirrings of the Spirit in many parts of the Republic these days, but how many of their compatriots in this country have been liberated from a superstitious, nominal Catholicism to a radiant faith in Christ?

(3) *The Southern Europeans* — the most prominent of these communities are:
(a) The 200,000 *Greek* speakers from Cyprus and Greece. The majority live in the London area. Greece shares with Malta the dubious distinction of having the smallest Evangelical witness of any land in free Europe. Although nominally Greek Orthodox, only 1% regularly go to church in Greece. The situation is little better among those living in the UK.

(b) The 200,000 *Italian* community scattered throughout Britain. Although Italy is a Catholic country, church attendances are low, anti-clericalism strong and occultism widely practised.

(4) *Muslims from the Middle East.* Islam has become prominent in Britain, and their missionary work to convert the country to Islam is extensive. There are over 500 mosques and 3,000 Koranic Schools in Britain today. We afford Muslims a privilege they deny Christians in their own lands. Opportunities to witness to tourists, students and immigrants from these 'closed' lands must be fully used. Three major groups are the Arabs (150,000 — including 12,000 Yemenis), Turks (55,000 from both Cyprus and Turkey — 40,000 in NE London), and, increasingly, Iranis. This is indeed a strategic mission field when one considers that an indigenous evangelical witness scarcely exists in Turkey, Cyprus, and most of the Arab lands of North Africa and the Middle East.

(5) *South Asians* come mainly from Pakistan, India and Bangladesh. They number some 1.4 million today — about 200,000 being from East Africa. The major ethno-linguistic groups are the Pakistanis (250,000 — almost all Muslims), Punjabis (300,000 — equal numbers of Sikhs and Hindus), Gujaratis (330,000 — about 70% Hindu, 30% Muslim) and Bengalis (ca. 190,000 — mainly Muslims from Bangladesh). The many references to this highly visible group of ethnic

minorities in this book and the obvious paucity of effort to reach them with the Gospel is a rebuke to us. Response to the Gospel has been very small among the Pakistanis and Punjabis, and virtually non-existent among the Gujaratis and Bengalis. Most of them come from the least evangelised parts of the Indian sub-continent. If vital, growing churches were planted in these communities, the effects would soon be felt in their lands of origin.

(6) *East Asians* are mainly Chinese. Ethnic Chinese total about 125,000 though some are classified in statistics as 'Vietnamese' because of their flight from that land. The large majority belong to a mixture of the various Chinese religions and Buddhism with a basic materialism predominating. Of these, about 2% would be Christians.

(7) *Africans* — about 85,000 from all over Anglophone Africa, and almost all living in London. Many are, at least nominally, Christian, but a minority are Muslims from Nigeria and other West African countries.

(8) *West Indians* are mostly black and speak English. Their number is reckoned to be about 1.1 million. As indicated in some of the questionnaire returns, and in various surveys, Christianity, especially in its evangelical/pentecostal form, is a more significant force among them than in any other community in the UK. They have their problems — many are poor and unemployed living in the inner cities and with the younger generation rejecting many of the values and the religion of their parents. However the many live West Indian churches should be sending out workers to preach the Gospel at home and abroad!

The strategic importance of these minorities
All but the last of these groups represent an enormous challenge to Christians in this country. Can we grasp the significance of this on a world-wide scale? Look again at the world diagram above. The 4 million or so 'new' British could be the evangelistic key for *hundreds of millions* of those of the same language and culture who have *never* heard the Gospel, and who are far more reachable by those of their number who become Christians in Britain. Even very small groups of people living in this country may provide

the key for Bible translation work, and preparing radio programmes, literature, cassettes, and video tapes to reach for totally unevangelised peoples who are inaccessible by any other than indirect means!

How can we neglect this part of the Great Commission — which is, in effect, our 'Samaria' (Acts 1:8)?

What ought we to do about this need?
There are enormous social, emotional, political, religious and psychological barriers on *both* sides to bringing the Gospel to the 'Samaritans' around us.

The 'new' British and our foreign visitors face many problems in our rather exclusive and prejudiced society. Some of these are well expressed in the questionnaire returns in this book — loneliness, lack of friends, difficulties in handling immigration formalities, health needs, a new language, our social welfare system, education, job-seeking, etc. All these give pre-evangelism contacts and opportunities for friendships to develop for those prepared to make the effort, that will earn them the right to share their faith in the Lord Jesus Christ.

In the 'old' British there is reserve, and fear of the unknown. We feel inadequate in coping with a different culture; we do not understand enough about other religions. We fear the consequences of exposing ourselves to costly investment of time and effort to build relationships and perhaps be hurt or rebuffed in the process. Yet for Jesus and for the Gospel we must. There is no other way but for ordinary Christians and ordinary congregations to reach out to these for whom the Saviour died. Love covers both a multitude of sins and also mistakes of approach!

This is not the place to develop ways and means of actually evangelising and discipling those of other cultures in our midst. There will always be problems — should we aim for separate ethnic churches or should we emphasise the unity of the Body of Christ which transcends culture? The experience of many in this type of outreach is that the first generation needs a separate cultural expression of the Church with only a minority of indigenous British involved directly; but subsequent generations may become more easily integrated. Dependence on the guidance of the Holy Spirit is needed in every case that the Gospel be best furthered here in Britain and overseas. The way to start is by earnest prayer for any cultural group in *your* area as *your* responsibility! This will lead to thrilling developments — so beware!

GRAND TOTALS

(for Wales, see page 140)

ENGLAND

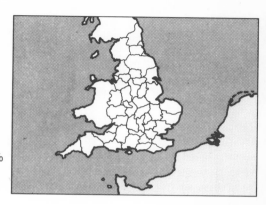

Total population: 46,804,000

Estimated number
attending church: 4,023,000

**Total number not regularly
attending church: 42,781,000**

Non-attenders as
percentage of population: 91%

Number of people not regularly attending church:

Age		Sex	
Under 15:	9,027,000	**Men:**	20,965,000
15-19:	3,427,000	**Women:**	21,816,000
20-29:	6,099,000		
30-44:	8,129,000		
45-64:	9,883,000		
65 or over:	6,216,000		

ENGLAND AND WALES

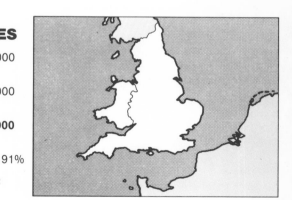

Total population: 49,613,000

Estimated number
attending church: 4,429,000

**Total number not regularly
attending church: 45,184,000**

Non-attenders as
percentage of population: 91%

Number of people not regularly attending church:

Age		Sex	
Under 15:	9,508,000	**Men:**	22,166,000
15-19:	3,619,000	**Women:**	23,018,000
20-29:	6,483,000		
30-44:	8,562,000		
45-64:	10,460,000		
65 or over:	6,552,000		

COUNTIES IN THE UK

The Unchurched
Those who do not go to any church

Less than 85% of population

85-89%

90% or more

COUNTY SUMMARY

Numbers are in thousands

	Total Population	Church Attenders	Non-Attenders	Under 15	15-19	20-29	30-44	45-64	Over 65	Men	Women
Avon	931	91	840	168	67	126	160	193	126	403	437
Bedfordshire	512	55	457	105	37	69	91	105	50	233	224
Berkshire	700	60	640	147	51	96	128	141	77	320	320
Buckinghamshire	581	55	526	116	42	79	105	121	63	263	263
Cambridgeshire	599	56	543	119	44	92	119	109	60	277	266
Cheshire	932	113	819	180	66	115	164	188	106	409	410
Cleveland	567	41	526	131	42	79	95	116	63	258	268
Cornwall and Isles of Scilly	430	41	389	78	31	58	70	90	62	191	198
Cumbria	483	58	425	85	34	55	81	106	64	208	217
Derbyshire	911	65	846	186	68	119	152	203	118	415	431
Devon	966	87	879	167	70	114	150	202	176	431	448
Dorset	605	69	536	96	37	75	86	129	113	252	284
Durham	608	51	557	122	45	78	106	128	78	273	284
East Sussex	671	77	594	101	47	83	101	137	125	273	321
Essex	1,484	122	1,362	313	109	191	272	300	177	667	695
Gloucestershire	506	53	453	104	36	63	82	100	68	222	231
Greater London	6,765	559	6,206	1,071	497	830	1,303	1,489	1,016	3,018	3,188
Greater Manchester	2,605	220	2,385	525	191	334	429	572	334	1,169	1,216
Hampshire	1,486	111	1,375	316	124	220	261	289	165	701	674
Hereford and Worcester	639	54	585	128	47	82	117	129	82	287	298
Hertfordshire	968	73	895	197	72	125	179	215	107	439	456
Humberside	856	45	811	187	65	113	146	187	113	397	414
Kent	1,486	110	1,376	316	110	193	248	303	206	674	702
Isle of Wight	119	12	107	20	7	13	17	27	23	50	57
Lancashire	1,384	157	1,227	270	98	160	221	282	196	589	638
Leicestershire	861	65	796	175	64	127	151	175	104	390	406
Lincolnsire	552	62	490	103	39	73	93	113	69	245	245
Merseyside	1,511	183	1,328	292	106	199	239	306	186	651	677
Norfolk	705	52	653	137	52	91	118	150	105	320	333
Northamptonshire	537	49	488	117	39	78	93	102	59	244	244
Northumberland	300	26	274	58	22	38	49	66	41	134	140
North Yorkshire	678	65	613	129	49	86	110	141	98	300	313
Nottinghamshire	991	61	930	205	74	130	177	214	130	456	474
Oxfordshire	548	47	501	106	45	85	105	100	60	266	235
Shropshire	380	32	348	77	28	49	66	76	52	171	177
Somerset	432	43	389	78	31	58	74	90	58	195	194
South Yorkshire	1,313	79	1,234	271	99	173	222	296	173	605	629
Staffordshire	1,019	78	941	217	75	141	188	217	103	461	480
Suffolk	611	59	552	116	39	83	110	121	83	276	276
Surrey	1,014	95	919	193	73	129	165	221	138	450	469
Tyne and Wear	1,150	86	1,064	223	85	160	192	255	149	511	553
Warwickshire	477	47	430	99	34	60	86	99	52	211	219
West Midlands	2,667	203	2,464	542	197	345	468	592	320	1,207	1,257
West Sussex	673	54	619	111	43	87	105	149	124	297	322
West Yorkshire	2,063	152	1,911	420	153	268	344	439	287	917	994
Wiltshire	528	50	478	110	43	77	91	100	57	239	239
All England	46,804	4,023	42,781	9.027	3,427	6,099	8,129	9,883	6,216	20,965	21,816
All Wales	2,809	406	2,403	481	192	384	433	577	336	1,201	1,202
England and Wales	49,613	4,429	45,184	9,508	3,619	6,483	8,562	10,460	6,552	22,166	23,018

Total population: 931,000

Estimated number attending church: 91,000

Total number not regularly attending church: 840,000

Non-attenders as percentage of population: 90%

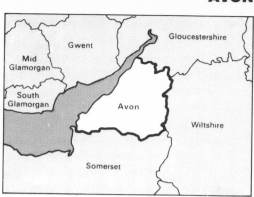

Number of people not regularly attending church:

Age		Sex	
Under 15:	168,000	**Men:**	403,000
15-19:	67,000	**Women:**	437,000
20-29:	126,000		
30-44:	160,000		
45-64:	193,000		
65 or over:	126,000		

SOCIAL/COMMUNITY GROUPS

	Description & Location	Characteristics	Openings for Outreach	Contact Person
S1	9/10,000 working men and women in the Filton area of Bristol mostly engaged in aircraft engineering. More men than women.	Working age range; all social classes, Anglican, Roman Catholic, Methodist and Baptist churches in the area.	5% Christian. Services of an Industrial Chaplain. Need pastoral care and a Christian point of reference.	n/a
S2	Council estate tenants in Bath — about 4,000 living in poorer areas, mostly labourers or unemployed. Men and women.	Social groups IV & V. Often insecure and unable to make commitments. Financial problems.	1% Christian. Contact with Evangelism Explosion teams and Sunday School.	Rev Alan Bain 39 Frome Road Odd Down Bath Avon BA2 2QF
S3	A project on a council estate in Bath for youth and family activities; about 240 involved — young people, cleaners, housewives, railway workers. Men and women.	Social groups III & V. Concerned with material needs and family problems. The Church does not seem relevant.	4% Christian. The Brethren are in contact.	n/a
S4	150-200 people living in a part of Stoke Hill, Bristol. A cross section of ages and includes doctors, solicitors, head teachers, shop owners.	Professional and management middle class. Their concerns are affluence, property, business, careers and education. Christianity appears irrelevant.	10% Christian. There are house groups run and the Church of England and Baptist Church are in contact.	Rev Canon Dr G L Carey Stoke Hill Bristol BS9 1BB
S5	Several hundred residents of old people's homes and in sheltered accommodation in the suburbs of Bristol. They have had various occupations in their past. Men and women.	They suffer from loneliness, depression and purposelessness and become very enclosed and alienated.	5% Christian. Fortnightly services are held by the Church of England and Baptist Church. Methodist Church is also in contact.	Rev P F Yacomeni 61 Fernsteed Road Bishopsworth Bristol BS13 8HE

AVON

ETHNIC/LINGUISTIC GROUPS

	Description & Location	Characteristics	Openings for Outreach	Contact Person
E1	A group of Rastafarians living in downtown inner city and council estates in Bristol. Mostly men in the 20-30 age group. Mainly unemployed.	Their background is originally Christian. They all speak English; some 80% would read it easily. Their response to the Church is a prejudice against orthodox religion and authority which is interpreted as white domination.	No known Christian outreach.	n/a

OCCASIONAL GROUPS

O1	A National Housewives' Register at Locking with 30 members. Women only; mainly young with families. They meet monthly.	Social groups II & III. They are conscious of their family responsibilities and their intellectual needs. They have a fear of Church commitment, and a lack of faith.	20% Christian. Occasional Christian speaker. Individual and personal opportunities for witness.	n/a
O2	40-60 members of local conjuring clubs. Men only meeting in Bath and Bristol fortnightly. All ages. 'Closed-shop' type of membership.	Employed in various jobs and no special social groups. Some magical practices not consistent with a Christian faith.	5% Christian at the most. Several attend church. Difficult to approach them as a group.	n/a
O3	About 50 vagrants in the city centre of Bristol. A mixed age range. Men and women. Some work washing up or as night watchmen.	Unskilled class. Seeking food, shelter and alcohol. They have a lack of purpose in life and are not aware of the Christian Gospel.	Possibly some are Christian. Direct evangelism has not been welcomed. Salvation Army, Roman Catholic and Methodist Churches in contact.	Rev Roy Allison Central Hall Old Market Street Bristol BS2 0HB
O4	A youth club with 100 members at Filton. All young people, many employed in engineering, at school or unemployed. Meet weekly.	Skilled manual or unskilled social classes. Their home backgrounds and lack of knowledge and consequent prejudice are blocks to the Gospel.	10% Christian. The Methodist Church runs the club and would value support, help and sympathy. The Roman Catholic Church and the Church of England are in the area.	n/a
O5	More than 50 members of a club for over 60s meeting weekly on a housing estate in Bristol. Men and women.	Unskilled social class. Problems are loneliness and widowhood. They consider they know all about Christianity.	5% Christian. The Baptist Church is in contact.	n/a
O6	100 in a Senior citizens' club at Locking, all retired. Men and women.	Social groups III, IV & V. Loneliness and missing out on a divine dimension. Fear of involvement with the Church.	20% Christian. The Church of England is in contact and the local Vicar visits.	n/a

Total population:	512,000
Estimated number attending church:	55,000
Total number not regularly attending church:	**457,000**
Non-attenders as percentage of population:	89%

Number of people not regularly attending church:

Age		Sex	
Under 15:	105,000	**Men:**	233,000
15-19:	37,000	**Women:**	224,000
20-29:	69,000		
30-44:	91,000		
45-64:	105,000		
65 or over:	50,000		

SOCIAL/COMMUNITY GROUPS

	Description & Location	Characteristics	Openings for Outreach	Contact Person
S1	People living on council estates at Leighton Buzzard. Majority are young, working in the sandpits, tile making and haulage. Men and women.	Social groups IV & V. Lack courage and fear that in joining a church they will make fools of themselves.	1% Christian. The Salvation Army have contact.	n/a
S2	5,000 living on a private housing estate at Dunstable, cover the complete age range. Most employed in clerical and engineering, some with responsibility. Men and women.	Social group III, non-manual. Most are self satisfied. Many have marital problems. Do not sense need for Gospel; are apathetic.	3% Christian. Undenominational evangelical church in contact. Door to door visitation on a regular basis.	Mr C G Rudd 17 Marina Drive Dunstable Beds. LU6 2AH

OCCASIONAL GROUPS

O1	A number of young married executives settled in private houses at Leighton Buzzard who commute to London. The majority are men employed in banks and business houses.	Social classes I & II. They meet after work in pubs and leisure centres. They do not have any sense of need. They are very conscious of their social position and culture. They would consider it a sign of weakness to be religious.	2% Christian. The Baptist Church is in contact. The Christians in the group try to reach out with friendship evangelism. Evangelism must be creative, fast moving and sincere.	Mr N C Barr 12 South Street Leighton Buzzard Beds. LU7 8NT

Description & Location	Characteristics	Openings for Outreach	Contact Person
O2 14 hardworking men and women between the ages of 25-60 who seek to work for others. All have a common interest in music. All living near Beaconsfield. They meet twice a week.	Social class II. Very conscious of the care of others and social concerns and their own insignificance. The dreariness of some church worship and the lack of professionalism in actions are blocks to the Gospel.	35% Christian. The Church of England is in contact. Church based social action.	n/a

Total population:	700,000
Estimated number attending church:	60,000
Total number not regularly attending church:	**640,000**
Non-attenders as percentage of population:	91%

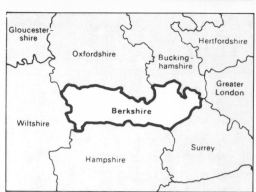

Number of people not regularly attending church:

Age		Sex	
Under 15:	147,000	**Men:**	320,000
15-19:	51,000	**Women:**	320,000
20-29:	96,000		
30-44:	128,000		
45-64:	141,000		
65 or over:	77,000		

SOCIAL/COMMUNITY GROUPS

	Description & Location	Characteristics	Openings for Outreach	Contact Person
S1	About 40 young families at Wraysbury. Many working at Heathrow.	Social groups III. Concern about future of the world but no real religious enquiry. Very considerable social life. The Church appears sterile and self-centred.	Two-thirds of the children in church are from non-church families. The Baptist Church is in contact.	Rev N V Pitts 21 Nelson Road Windsor Berks. SL4 3RQ
S2	40 established villagers living in council houses or unrestored cottages near Hungerford. Men and women.	All manual, skilled or unskilled workers. Recent newcomers in village taking over the Church.	1 church member. Anglican Church contact with Vicar.	n/a

ETHNIC/LINGUISTIC GROUPS

E1	20,000 people of Asian origin living in and around Slough with a heavy concentration at Chalvey. From India, Pakistan, and East Africa. Many working in light industry on a local trading estate. They have lived in the area for some 20 years.	60% read English. Mother tongue mainly Punjabi. The majority are Muslim. Some are Sikh and Hindu. They are conscious of their material needs and a need to be accepted as equals in the community. Their religious background and apathy are blocks to the Gospel.	Less than 1% Christian. One full time missionary based at St Paul's Chalvey. The BCMS are active.	Miss J Millson 8 Lawkland Farnham Royal Slough Berks. SL2 3AN *and* Mr Keith Moyes 19 Lascelles Road Slough Berks. SL3 7PN

BERKSHIRE

Description & Location	Characteristics	Openings for Outreach	Contact Person
O1 Workers attending social clubs around Reading. Their work ranges from labouring to clerical. Each club would have an approximate membership of 100 men and women.	Social classes IV & V. Conscious of social needs and have difficulty in seeing the relevance of the Lord in their daily lives.	Number of Christians not known. Anglican Church is in contact through campaigns and visitation. Pentecostal and Baptist Churches also present in area.	Mr John A Wicks 22 St Michael's Road Tilehurst Reading Berks. RG3 4RP
O2 All people connected with horse racing in the Newbury area. Trainers and staff and jockeys and those involved in the betting business. All ages. Men and women.	Covers members of most social classes. They are absorbed by the excitement of racing. Their self-satisfaction and the Church's lack of imaginative outreach are blocks to the Gospel.	Number of Christians not known. Very little outreach at present. Churches of various denominations in the area.	Rev Alison Overton 4 Bartlemy Road Newbury Berks. RG14 6JX

BUCKINGHAMSHIRE

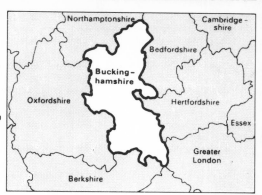

Total population:	581,000
Estimated number attending church:	55,000
Total number not regularly attending church:	**526,000**
Non-attenders as percentage of population:	91%

Number of people not regularly attending church:

Age		Sex	
Under 15:	116,000	**Men:**	263,000
15-19:	42,000	**Women:**	263,000
20-29:	79,000		
30-44:	105,000		
45-64:	121,000		
65 or over:	63,000		

SOCIAL/COMMUNITY GROUPS

	Description & Location	Characteristics	Openings for Outreach	Contact Person
S1	Inhabitants of a village near Aylesbury; population 800. Most are financially solvent; half owner-occupiers, half tenants. Men and women of all ages.	Social groups I, II, III, & IV. Business men, farm and factory workers. They would see their needs as financial. The Gospel does not seem relevant to them.	700 do not attend church. Anglican and Methodist Churches have contact.	Rev T M Thorp The Vicarage Whitchurch Aylesbury Bucks HP22 4JZ
S2	2,000 men and women in the Hughenden Valley. Occupied in BBC, furniture trade and as carpenters. All ages.	Management social group. Comfortable and well-off. Materialism is a block to the Good News. They are conscious of community needs.	3% are Christian. The Church of England and Methodist Church are present. Christian outreach possible through Meals on Wheels, Young Wives Groups, OAP Clubs and Youth Organisations.	n/a
S3	About 2.5% of the population of Stony Stratford. Men and women, ages 18-25 working in the transport industry: buses, road haulage and railways.	Social class IV. Shift work tends to isolate them socially.	Very few Christians. A local study showed they had a high awareness of the Christian message but low contact with the Church.	n/a

ETHNIC/LINGUISTIC GROUPS

E1	A small Gipsy encampment with some 30 caravans west of Milton Keynes. Other travellers join the camp particularly in the Autumn.	Only a small number read English easily. Their mother tongue is Romany. Their religion is not known. They are sometimes hostile to outsiders and they have literacy problems.	No known Christians. Some have attended the local church out of curiosity.	n/a

BUCKINGHAMSHIRE

	Description & Location	Characteristics	Openings for Outreach	Contact Person
O1	A group from 76 houses at Aston Clinton formed into an informal residents' association with common interests and social status. Men and women, mostly aged 30-45, with young families.	Middle-management; self-employed business men and women. They are concerned with promotion at work, material improvement and education of their children. Their life-style is a block to the Good News.	4% Christian. United Mission Aylesbury, Home groups and the Baptist Church all involved in outreach. The Church of England and the Roman Catholic Church also in contact.	n/a
O2	A youth club of over 50 boys and girls meeting weekly at Quainton. School children with their leaders.	Very conscious of social needs — for example, staging special events. The club leaders are reluctant to allow Bible teachers to influence their club.	5% Christian. The Church of England is in contact.	n/a
O3	700 office workers in an establishment at High Wycombe. Men and women, age range 20-35. All employed in clerical or executive work.	Professional social status. Conscious of material needs. Their wealth, apathy and independence cut them off from the Gospel.	5-10% Christian. A small group meets weekly for worship. A Chaplain, articles in office magazine, literature would all offer openings for outreach.	n/a
04	A group of 20 people employed as MOD police and living on council estates at Westcott. All ages.	Social group III, non-manual. There is a lack of interest in the Gospel and a contentment with material things.	1 Christian. Personal witness only. There is a Church of England church in the village.	n/a

Total population: 599,000

Estimated number
attending church: 56,000

**Total number not regularly
attending church: 543,000**

Non-attenders as
percentage of population: 91%

Number of people not regularly attending church:

Age		Sex	
Under 15:	119,000	**Men:**	277,000
15-19:	44,000	**Women:**	266,000
20-29:	92,000		
30-44:	119,000		
45-64:	109,000		
65 or over:	60,000		

SOCIAL/COMMUNITY GROUPS

	Description & Location	Characteristics	Openings for Outreach	Contact Person
S1	3,000 men and women living in semi-detached and detached houses on an estate in Peterborough. Most employed in insurance, teaching and building management.	Social classes I, II & III. They are primarily concerned with financial security. Their self-sufficiency and materialism are blocks to the Good News.	5% Christian. An area team from the Parish church is in contact on a small scale.	n/a
S2	A council estate at Sawston. 1,000 men and women of all ages, most employed as factory workers.	Social classes III & IV. They feel a need for help in times of crisis. They perceive the church is irrelevant and inhospitable. It appears to be for better-off people.	1-2% Christian. There are regular outreach activities.	n/a
S3	5,000 Londoners now living on an estate at Huntingdon, employed in local light industry — full age range. Men and women.	Semi-skilled workers concerned with material needs and social deprivation. They have a different culture to local Christians.	1% Christian. Two small free churches and Roman Catholics in contact.	Mr K Barnard 22 Hamlet Close Hartford Cambs PE18 7PD
S4	An estate on a suburb of Arbury, Cambridge. 1,000 residents working in factories and cleaning jobs. Some are unemployed, others self-employed. Men and women.	Social class V. Unemployment, family breakdown and lack of love are the main areas of need. They need a Gospel which responds to all their needs as whole people.	Number of Christians not known. The Baptists have a church and there is a Brethren Chapel.	Rev M Travers 258 Hills Road Cambridge CB2 2QE

	Description & Location	Characteristics	Openings for Outreach	Contact Person
S5	About 200 long established villagers in Kimbolton. Living mostly at one end of the village. Mainly older men and women. Many of the women work in school kitchens, as cleaners, domestic helps and shop assistants.	Adapting to a much changed social environment. Social groups III, IV & V. Concerned with good works. Little sense of spiritual need. Perhaps some are walking with Christ without knowing it; as in Emmaus.	Many nominal Christians; few committed. Evangelicals. The Church of England lay workers are active.	n/a
S6	540 on a housing estate 20 years old on the edge of an established village community at Histon. Men and women of all ages but many under 40. Office workers in town and University.	Non-manual office workers. Concerned with possessions, housing and children's education. They have little contact with Christians and the Church seems irrelevant.	10% Christian. No church on estate. Baptists and Anglicans have contact.	Mr A R Barker 2 Poplar Road Histon Cambs CB4 4LN
S7	3,000 University Research students at Cambridge. Men and women aged 22-26.	Professional social class. Loneliness, work pressures and a search for employment are their main concerns. Pressures of work and intellectual pride cut them off from Gospel.	5-7% Christian. Local Church of England and University Christian Union in contact.	Canon Mark Ruston 37 Jesus Lane Cambridge CB5 8BW
S8	1,200 men and women on a housing estate in Ely. Many are lorry drivers and factory workers.	Social class IV. Their preoccupations are financial. The Gospel doesn't appear relevant.	$1/2$% Christian. There are no churches and no outreach among them.	n/a

ETHNIC/LINGUISTIC GROUPS

	Description & Location	Characteristics	Openings for Outreach	Contact Person
E1	300 West Indians born in this country are concentrated in the Mill Road area of Cambridge. Mixed employment with some women in the nursing services.	90% read English which is the mother tongue. Their needs are various and there are many blocks to the Good News.	15% Christian. Many are Baptists or Pentecostal. Pastoral and evangelistic visiting offer a means of outreach.	Rev G Tubbs 61 Litchfield Road Cambridge CB1 3SP

OCCASIONAL GROUPS

	Description & Location	Characteristics	Openings for Outreach	Contact Person
O1	200 men and women in the age range 20-40 employed as salesmen, craftsmen or in the police, living at Bar Hill and members of the social clubs.	Social status II. Main concerns are a secure job, money to pay the mortgage and a happy family life. They feel that the church is irrelevant. Material concerns cut them off from the Gospel.	2% Christian. There is a local parish church and an Evangelical church.	n/a

	Description & Location	Characteristics	Openings for Outreach	Contact Person
O2	Social club at Witchford with 100/200 members concerned with the life of the village — often holds functions on Sundays. Men and women. Club includes youth activities. Mostly employed in agriculture.	Social groups III, IV & V. Apathy, unbelief and materialism are barriers to the Good News.	Some home meetings and the Baptist Church is in contact.	Rev David Ellis 53 London Road Chatteris Cambs PE16 6NW
O3	45 parents of a pre-school play group meeting 3 times a week at Cambridge. They work in the University in teaching and research.	Concerned with employment prospects and finance. Intellectual pride is a bar to Christianity.	10% Christian. The Church of England is in contact.	Canon Mark Ruston 37 Jesus Lane Cambridge CB5 8BW
O4	A Women's Institute in a village near Cambridge. Mainly elderly housewives. They meet monthly.	Very mixed backgrounds. Their common interest is friendship. They have no sense of need of the Gospel.	3% Christian. The few Christians witness to the others. There are local Church of England and URC Churches.	n/a

CHESHIRE

Total population:	932,000
Estimated number attending church:	113,000
Total number not regularly attending church:	**819,000**
Non-attenders as percentage of population:	88%

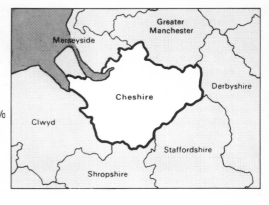

Number of people not regularly attending church:

Age		Sex	
Under 15:	180,000	**Men:**	409,000
15-19:	66,000	**Women:**	410,000
20-29:	115,000		
30-44:	164,000		
45-64:	188,000		
65 or over:	106,000		

SOCIAL/COMMUNITY GROUPS

	Description & Location	Characteristics	Openings for Outreach	Contact Person
S1	A group made up of 4,000 young marrieds and their families in the village of Hartford outside Northwich. Bound together by their social standing.	Social classes I, II & III. They have little sense of need and see the Church as irrelevant.	Not many Christians. Hartford parish church undertaking outreach. Times of crisis, like bereavement, present an opportunity.	Rev M P Marshall The Vicarage Hartford Northwich Cheshire CH8 1QQ
S2	A group of 2,000 people in the Crompton Road area of Macclesfield. Mainly elderly folk and young families. A wide range of types of employment.	Non-Manual, Skilled Manual and Semi-Skilled workers. They are concerned with self-fulfilment and find the Church remote and disinterested.	Up to 2% Christian. Anglican, Methodist and Roman Catholic Church have contact. Holiday clubs, Mums & Toddlers, Club for over 60s and children's work provide opportunities.	Mr John Staley 261 Oxford Road Macclesfield Cheshire SK11 8JY
S3	5,000 people living in Heaton Moor in Stockport. They are mainly young families with children. They work as bank officials, managers, in manufacturing or are self-employed.	Social classes I & II. The group is conscious of their status and their need to maintain it.	8-10% Christian. Roman Catholic, Church of England, Methodist and URC all present. Note that the Mormons and Jehovah's Witnesses are active.	Mr E N Taylor 42 Lea Road Stockport Cheshire SK4 4JU
S4	10-15,000 residents of Council Housing Estates in Ellesmere Port. Most would be unemployed.	Mainly social class V. Lack of faith and hope. Low achievement, low expectations and the popular media cut them off from the Gospel.	2-3% are Christians. There are several churches in the area. The Church of England and the Roman Catholic Churches have most contact.	n/a

	Description & Location	Characteristics	Openings for Outreach	Contact Person
S5	A group of 500 newcomers 'Dormitory Residents' at Bunbury. Mostly young parents. Many school age children. Parents employed by ICI and Shell.	Social groups IV & V. Lack of interest in the church, and rootlessness because their residence is not permanent.	5% Christian. Methodists and Church of England in contact.	n/a
S6	3,000 residents of a council estate at Lymm, in various occupations. Men and women.	Social classes III, IV & V. Main concern is unemployment. They see the Church as middle class.	5% Christian. Church of England and Roman Catholics, Baptists, Methodists, all have churches.	Rev P Pearson 16 Brook Road Lymm Cheshire WA13 9AH
S7	9,000 people near the town centre of Widnes. Mostly younger and mainly unemployed.	Social group V. Many were baptised RC but now they have no connection. Their main worry is financial. They tend to be very dependent on Social Services.	There are Church of England visitations and open air services.	n/a

ETHNIC/LINGUISTIC GROUPS

	Description & Location	Characteristics	Openings for Outreach	Contact Person
E1	Several thousand Jewish men and women in Altrincham.	All read English. English is their mother tongue; some learn Hebrew. Their religion is Judaism.	No known outreach.	Rev Dr P Beasley-Murray 43 Hale Road Altrincham Cheshire WA15 9HP
E2	100 Uganda Asians settled in Chester in the mid 70's after Amin's purge. Mainly young families with adults working in restaurants and take-aways.	All read English. Their mother tongue is Ugandan and religion Muslim. They are quite affluent. Their independence tends to cut them off from the Gospel.	No known outreach.	n/a
E3	A number of older Welsh men and women living in Chester. Many now work in the teaching or legal professions. Originally, their families came some 100 years ago to work on the railways.	40% Christian. Most would be Presbyterian. The group is conscious of cultural needs.	A little outreach. Church members in the group do welcome others.	Rev R Jones 6 Belgrave Road Boughton Heath Cheshire CH3 5SB

OCCASIONAL GROUPS

	Description & Location	Characteristics	Openings for Outreach	Contact Person
O1	An old people's club at Bickerton. 60 men and women who meet fortnightly. Some still do odd jobs; mostly retired.	Social class IV. The group feels a need to meet socially. Perhaps their age, familiarity with the Gospel and nominal Christianity cut them off from real faith.	Both the Anglican and Methodist Churches are active in the area. There are annual services for this group and they are invited to others.	Rev G Baines The Manse Brownknowl Broxton Chester CH3 9JU

Description & Location	Characteristics	Openings for Outreach	Contact Person
O2 A group of 50-70 physically handicapped men and women who meet in Bramhall for mutual support. They are working mainly in sheltered employment.	Social class IV. The group feels the need of support services. They tend to be more aware of temporal needs than spiritual needs.	10% Christian. There is pastoral concern on a limited level. Baptist and Congregational Churches present.	Mr Alan N Camp 35 South Parade Bramhall Stockport Cheshire SK7 3BJ
O3 60 young housewives, members of a Mother and Baby Club.	Social classes IV & V. Conscious of shortage of money, need for friends, opportunities for sharing news and concerns. There are several possible barriers to the Gospel: ignorance of the Good News, previous less than sensitive evangelism, family hostility and fear of involvement.	5% Christian. Methodist and Anglican churches active. Little direct Christian outreach.	n/a
O4 A Karate club in Stockport with 150-200 members. Men and women, 12-40 age range. All types of employment.	Mainly semi-skilled social class. Little sense of general need. Apathetic and self-involved, so the Gospel seems irrelevant.	1-2% Christian. Club meets in Church premises. Baptist and Congregational Churches in area.	Mr Alan N Camp 35 South Parade Bramhall Stockport Cheshire SK7 3BJ
O5 A group of 20 men and women at Warrington seeking to set up a hospice for the terminally ill. Doctors, architects, nurses and pharmacists.	They see their needs as primarily social. Yet their riches and social status cut them off from the Good News.	5% Christian. Local vicar undertaking outreach.	n/a

Total population: 567,000

Estimated number
attending church: 41,000

**Total number not regularly
attending church: 526,000**

Non-attenders as
percentage of population: 93%

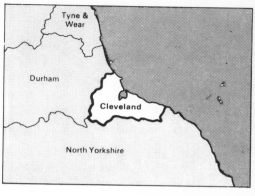

Number of people not regularly attending church:

Age		Sex	
Under 15:	131,000	**Men:**	258,000
15-19:	42,000	**Women:**	268,000
20-29:	79,000		
30-44:	95,000		
45-64:	116,000		
65 or over:	63,000		

SOCIAL/COMMUNITY GROUPS

	Description & Location	Characteristics	Openings for Outreach	Contact Person
S1	7,000 Council house tenants in an area of Stockton-on-Tees. Men and women. A growing number of young people and single-parent families. Many labourers, process workers and workers in the steel and engineering trades.	Semi-skilled and unskilled social classes. Many are unemployed. Working men's clubs are a meeting point. Many have a Roman Catholic background. There is a need for security and a sense of self-worth. The Church is perceived as irrelevant and church-going a sign of weakness.	2% Christian. Baptist Church only church in the area.	Rev R Searle The Manse 39 Trent Street Stockton-on-Tees TS20 2DP
S2	A group of some 45 young unemployed school leavers in Hartlepool. They live in the centre of the town in flats developed in the 1960's. A few have worked for a short time on Youth Training Schemes.	Mostly unskilled. Money is one of their main preoccupations. They escape from their situation through sex, drink, solvent abuse and vandalism.	None are Christian. The FIEC and Baptist are present. The Church of England has most impact. The local Curate acts as a youth worker and there is a Sunday evening drop-in centre.	Rev M Jennett Stranton Vicarage Westbourne Road Hartlepool Cleveland TS25 5RE
S3	About 1,200 unemployed young men and women in Saltburn.	Social groups III, IV & V. Needing work and feeling the loss of status. All have financial worries.	A few Christians. The Methodist Church is the most active.	n/a

Description & Location	Characteristics	Openings for Outreach	Contact Person
S4 3,000 unemployed young people at Stockton-on-Tees. Ages 17-21. Many from a council estate. Some have been on 6 months' work experience.	Social class V. Some would like employment, others have lost all desire to work. They cannot see that the Church is relevant to them. Peer group pressure also keeps them from the Church.	$^1/_2$% Christian. There are Christians working in the YMCA.	Rev R Searle The Manse 39 Trent Street Stockton-on-Tees Cleveland TS20 2DP

Total population: 430,000

Estimated number attending church: 41,000

Total number not regularly attending church: 389,000

Non-attenders as percentage of population: 90%

Number of people not regularly attending church:

Age		Sex	
Under 15:	78,000	**Men:**	191,000
15-19:	31,000	**Women:**	198,000
20-29:	58,000		
30-44:	70,000		
45-64:	90,000		
65 or over:	62,000		

SOCIAL/COMMUNITY GROUPS

	Description & Location	Characteristics	Openings for Outreach	Contact Person
S1	Inhabitants of a village council estate near Truro. 111 adults on electoral register and some 30 children. Wide age range. Mainly unemployed or working for the local authority.	Mainly semi-skilled. The Church does not seem culturally relevant.	3% Christian. Christian work among the children. Local Church of England at work.	n/a
S2	800 workers in a factory near Camborne. Men and women of all ages.	Skilled manual workers whose needs are social and financial. Indifference, apathy and materialism keep them from the Gospel.	5% Christian. There is individual witness and the Anglicans and Methodists have churches in the area.	n/a
S3	Some 400 retired folk, all older people living in bungalows on an attractive estate in Porthtowan. More women than men. They form about ⅓ of the village population.	Professional and management class. They tend to be self centred. Apathy and materialism are bars to the Gospel and God seems irrelevant to their pleasurable lifestyle.	8% Christian. Visitation by Christians over a long period from the Methodist Chapel. There is an Anglican church in the next village.	Mr Andrew Chapple Sunnymede Cottage Porthfowan Truro Cornwall TR4 8AY
S4	2,000 people living in bungalow developments on the outskirts of Helston. All retired; more women than men. They are English folk who have moved into the area after retiring some 10 years ago.	They are well-off and tend to keep to themselves until one partner dies.	There is a Parish church. Number of Christians not known. Many nominal Christians.	n/a

	Description & Location	Characteristics	Openings for Outreach	Contact Person
S5	5,500 Cornish folk in Camborne. Mainly younger people; more men than women. Generally mining and factory workers. They live in the town and suburbs particularly on council estates.	The security of their future is a worry particularly with high unemployment. The traditionalism of the Church and dull services separate them from the Gospel. Their religious background is Christianity and Celtic folklore.	2% Christian. The local Methodist Chapel is undertaking outreach. Youth for Christ are active and there is work among young Mums.	Rev N J Polock 17 Pendaries Road Camborne Cornwall TR14 7QB
S6	Residents living on a privately owned housing estate at Helston. Young men and women working at Culdrose Air Station as pilots, mechanics and maintenance staff.	Social groups III. The group tends to be involved in its own activities. The Church does not attract them.	There is a local Catholic Church as well as a local Parish Church. More attractive Sunday Schools could provide an opportunity for outreach. Jehovah's Witnesses and Mormons also active in the area.	Mrs D J Timmins Fermoy 38 Manor Way Gwealdues Helston Cornwall TR13 8LJ
S7	2,500 naval personnel and their families at Helston. Young folk working in the Services or engineering.	Conscious of few needs. Very high incidence of marital breakdown. They have a total lack of contact with Christian Church and little understanding of the Christian faith.	2% Christian. There are Church of England, Methodist and Roman Catholic Chaplains. There are also fellowship groups.	n/a
S8	The physically, socially and mentally handicapped of Wadebridge and district. At least 60; but probably more. Men and women, mainly elderly. None are employed.	Social class IV & V. They often have a sense of hopelessness and loneliness. Their needs are met by friendship, social contact, mobility and practical help.	15% Christian. The Methodists have most contact. A team of Christians run a coffee bar and mobilise community resources to bring them together. There are also Pastoral counsellors available.	Mr R G G Stevenson Runnymede Fernleigh Road Wadebridge Cornwall PL27 7AZ

OCCASIONAL GROUPS

O1	Groups catering for retired men — Probus clubs at Newquay, 2 groups with a total membership of 80.	Satisfaction and financial security are blocks to the Gospel. Increasing age and problems of retirement are their many preoccupations.	30% Christian. Church of England and Methodists have most contact with group.	n/a

Total population: 483,000

Estimated number attending church: 58,000

Total number not regularly attending church: 425,000

Non-attenders as percentage of population: 88%

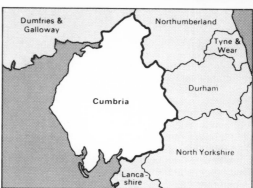

Number of people not regularly attending church:

Age		Sex	
Under 15:	85,000	**Men:**	208,000
15-19:	34,000	**Women:**	217,000
20-29:	55,000		
30-44:	81,000		
45-64:	106,000		
65 or over:	64,000		

SOCIAL/COMMUNITY GROUPS

	Description & Location	Characteristics	Openings for Outreach	Contact Person
S1	Housing estate on the edge of the market town of Kendal. 1,500-2,000 men and women of all ages.	Mostly skilled and manual workers — some unskilled. Some feel lonely. Materialism and indifference to spiritual needs cut them off from the Gospel.	1% Christian. Regular visiting by Anglican Church.	Canon R G Forward St Thomas Vicarage Queen's Road Kendal Cumbria LA9 4PL
S2	30,000 men and women of all ages in and around the market town of Kendal in various types of employment.	Social class III. Conscious of the need for security but have a lack of knowledge of sin.	1% Christian. Church of England, Brethren and Methodist churches all have contacts.	Mr G J Hobson Lingrue Mount Pleasant Arnside Carnforth LA5 0EX
S3	A council estate near Workington. 1,200 factory workers. Mainly older men and women.	Social groups IV & V. Conscious of a lack of social cohesion. The main blocks to their knowledge of God is individualism and lack of evangelism and Christian education.	The number of Christians is not known. Only a Church of England church in the area. Visitation by church members.	n/a
S4	About 200 travellers staying on a local travellers' site known as Bleak House. Most are young. Only working occasionally in buying and selling.	Social groups IV & V. Their children are important to them. Their care for each other cuts them off from outreach.	The Roman Catholic Church has contact with the children. Baptisms, first communions, marriages and funerals present opportunities for outreach.	Fr W Walsh St Catherine's Droves Lane Penrith CA11 9EL

CUMBRIA

OCCASIONAL GROUPS

Description & Location	Characteristics	Openings for Outreach	Contact Person
O1 More than 60 men and women in a local social club at Kirkby Stephen. They meet most evenings. Most live on a council estate. They are middle aged to elderly working as labourers, council workers, trades people and local craftsmen.	Social groups III, IV & V. Concerned with social enjoyment. They are ignorant of God's love and ways and dislike formal religion.	The Anglican, Roman Catholic and Methodist churches all have tenuous links. Regular home visitation would provide a means of outreach.	Mr B Umpleby 50 South Road Kirkby Stephen Cumbria CA17 4SN
O2 Group of 15 young mothers who meet at a playgroup and toddler group, using church premises in Barrow-in-Furness. Husbands work in shipbuilding and engineering.	Their needs are to share news and experiences with each other. They are disinterested in the Church.	No known Christian contact.	Rev C Gillhespey The Rectory 98 Roose Road Barrow-in-Furness Cumbria LA13 9RL

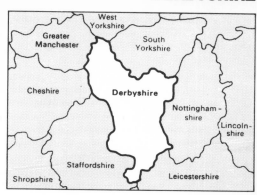

Total population:	911,000
Estimated number attending church:	65,000
Total number not regularly attending church:	**846,000**
Non-attenders as percentage of population:	93%

Number of people not regularly attending church:

Age		Sex	
Under 15:	186,000	**Men:**	415,000
15-19:	68,000	**Women:**	431,000
20-29:	119,000		
30-44:	152,000		
45-64:	203,000		
65 or over:	118,000		

SOCIAL/COMMUNITY GROUPS

	Description & Location	Characteristics	Openings for Outreach	Contact Person
S1	The Village of Tibshelf. Population of 3,100. Men and women of all ages. Strong links with the mining industry. ¼ of the workforce work for the NCB.	All social classes. Most would see their needs as material and emotional. Ignorance of the Gospel, the weakness of the Church and the grip of the Evil One keep them from Christ.	3% Christian. Three churches and a House Fellowship in the area.	Mr G Campbell The Vicarage 67 High Street Tibshelf Derby DE5 5NU
S2	Numbers of coalminers living in and around Swanwick. Most are married men.	Skilled manual workers, attending church only on special occasions. Class and shiftwork make churchgoing difficult.	The Non-conformist churches have more contact with this group. Baptisms and marriages are an opportunity for outreach.	Rev P Vessey St Andrews Vicarage Broadway Swanwick DE55 1DQ
S3	8,000 men and women living in Swacetown. They tend to live in council houses. Many are unemployed. Others work as coal miners and foundry workers.	Skilled Manual and Semi-Skilled workers. They turn to the Church at times of rites of passage. Would not like to be thought of as non-Christian.	1% Christian. Church of England and Methodist churches present.	Rev J C Render 46 Thanet Street Clay Cross Chesterfield S45 9JT
S4	A group of 3,000 living on a private housing estate at Swanwick, employed in commuter jobs: teaching, insurance and middle management.	Social Groups I & III. Their needs are friendship, practical help and community life. Busy lives, ambition at work and leisure activities are blocks to the Good News.	3% Christian. There are churches in the area.	Rev Dr R G Harris 19 Hickton Road Swanwick Derby DE55 1DQ

	Description & Location	Characteristics	Openings for Outreach	Contact Person
S5	10,000 men and women of all ages, mainly council house tenants, living in North Wingfield, a village outside Chesterfield. Most working in mining, as bus drivers or shop workers.	Social group IV. The areas of jobs and money are a source of preoccupation. They do not appear to be interested in the Church.	1-5% Christian. Door to door visitation, Easter pageant in the streets and a free Christian newspaper are all means of outreach. There are Anglican and Pentecostal Churches locally.	Ms Anne Scott 76 The Green Hasland Chesterfield S41 0JU
S6	Community of 5,000 living at Duffield and employed mainly by British Rail or Rolls Royce. Men and women. Many young people.	Main concerns are career, paying the mortgage and good education for the children. Self-sufficiency keeps them from the Gospel and they see religion, especially the Church, as irrelevant.	10-15% Christian. All churches engage in a degree of outreach. Anglicans, Baptists, Methodists and Roman Catholics all have churches.	Rev A G MacKenzie 21 Castle Hill Duffield Derbyshire DE6 4EA
S7	A group of working class folk including young marrieds, single people, marrieds and retired old folk, all numbering 6,000 and living in an inner suburb of Derby. Most are employed on the shop floor or in manual work on the railways or in engineering.	Social groups III & IV. Concerned with material things and self-sufficiency. They consider the Church to be irrelevant to their general everyday needs but would contact the Church for christenings, marriages and funerals.	2% Christian. There are Anglican and Methodist churches and both are in contact through church activities such as Young Wives Groups, Old Folks Groups and care for the poor in the community, particularly one-parent families.	n/a
S8	5,000 men and women of all ages living in Swadlincote, 3 mining villages grown into one town of 20,000 people. Most would work in coal mining or related industries.	Social groups III & IV. They are not conscious of any needs.	1% Christian. The Methodist Church and the Anglican Church have the most impact. The Baptist Church is also present. Mums and Toddlers groups and Playgroups are a means of outreach.	Rev H J Heybur 76 Hartshorne Road Woodville Nr Burton-on-Trent Staffs DE11 7HZ

ETHNIC/LINGUISTIC GROUPS

E1	Several thousands of Asian immigrants at Derby in the Pear Tree/ Normanton districts from India and Pakistan. They are employed in all kinds of work: labouring, and some in business or shopkeeping. Rolls Royce and British Rail are large employers.	Some 40%, predominantly men, read English easily. The native languages are Urdu, Gujarati and Punjabi. There are many Sikhs, Moslems and Hindus. They are deeply entrenched in their own faith and national-cultural aspirations.	There are very few Christians. There is an Asian minister and his wife undertaking evangelism.	Rev H Nuttall 155 Almond Street Derby DE3 6LY

OCCASIONAL GROUPS

	Description & Location	Characteristics	Openings for Outreach	Contact Person
O1	50-100 rural agricultural workers in the area of Dale Abbey, Stanton-by-Dale and Ilkeston. They come together infrequently.	Skilled Manual and Semi-skilled workers. Main concern is a secure future. God is still part of their folklore but tends to be more relevant at Harvest time.	5% Christian. There is a local Church of England and the Rector visits. A Chaplaincy type ministry could be effective.	Rev I E Godding The Rectory Stanton-by-Dale Ilkeston Derbyshire DE7 4QA
O2	About 100 mothers with young children in a Mums and Toddlers Group and Playgroup in Chesterfield. Some do clerical work, or some shift work.	Group II social class. Most would be concerned with the upbringing of their children. The Church is seen to be socially active but its motivation is not always clear.	5-10% Christian. The Methodist Church is active, holding special services and running discussion groups and a coffee shop.	Rev M S Stillwell 39 Broomfield Ave Hasland Chesterfield S41 4LU

DEVON

Total population:	966,000
Estimated number attending church:	87,000
Total number not regularly attending church:	**879,000**
Non-attenders as percentage of population:	91%

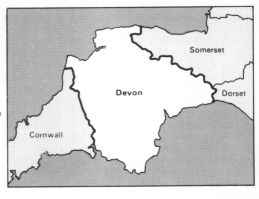

Number of people not regularly attending church:

Age		Sex	
Under 15:	167,000	**Men:**	431,000
15-19:	70,000	**Women:**	448,000
20-29:	114,000		
30-44:	150,000		
45-64:	202,000		
65 or over:	176,000		

SOCIAL/COMMUNITY GROUPS

	Description & Location	Characteristics	Openings for Outreach	Contact Person
S1	About 4,000 people on a 25-year-old council estate in Exeter. All have a similar lifestyle. Varied employment, mostly semi-skilled. All ages.	Social class IV. See church as irrelevant.	1-2% Christian. Anglican and Brethren ministry but impact is small.	n/a
S2	About 500 farmers and farm workers scattered over a large area around Honiton. They meet for whist drives and dances. Many elderly.	Social class II and IV. The nature of their work makes it difficult to attend church. Usual needs of remote rural areas.	90% nominal Christian. Anglican and Baptist churches in the area. There is a need for special times for services.	Mr T Gibbins Ottermead Upottery Honiton E Devon EX14 9NF
S3	A group of 400 engaged in the fishing industry with their families, living at Brixham.	Social groups III, IV & V. A variety of work all connected with fishing and boats. The church does not relate to their lifestyle.	2% Christian. Baptist, Methodist RC and Anglican churches in the area, also a connection with the RNMDSF.	n/a
S4	400 young families on new estate at Cullompton. Police, salesmen and lower management, all with similar incomes.	Social class II & III. See no need for faith.	3% Christian. Anglican, Baptist and Christian Brethren churches in the area. Coffee mornings are held and visitation.	Mr A D Charters White Lodge 7 New Street Cullompton Devon EX15 1HA
S5	About 400 people living in sea-front residences at Plymouth. Mostly engaged in hotel business or bed and breakfast.	Social class II. Often concerned about the unpredictability of tourist trade. They have difficulty in getting to services because of work.	Very few Christians. Church of England visiting and outreach through the children	n/a

	Description & Location	Characteristics	Openings for Outreach	Contact Person
S6	Groups of about 25 older people to be found in most villages of North Devon. Retired agricultural workers.	Semi-skilled. Many are very lonely and need friendship and interest. Those who do not attend church do not see it as relevant.	30% Christian. There are Anglican, Methodist and URC churches in the area.	n/a

OCCASIONAL GROUPS

	Description & Location	Characteristics	Openings for Outreach	Contact Person
O1	Between 50 and 120 elderly and retired people at Torbay meeting in an Over 60s club.	All social classes. They are very conscious of death, loneliness and illness. Many feel that living a 'good life' removes need for faith.	30% Christian. Most denominations in the area.	n/a
O2	About 50 members of the Old Age Pensioners Federation at Plymouth. Retired dockyard workers, fitters, turners and postmen and their wives.	Social class III & IV. Maybe bored and lonely. There is a need for a community centre. They do not see the relevance of church.	Anglican contact.	Rev E Summers St Barnabas Vicarage 10 De La Hay Ave, Plymouth PL34 1TU
O3	About 60 people, mostly men, at Crediton. A club dedicated to community work. Mainly middle aged, bankers and businessmen.	Social class I, II & III. They do good works which gives them a sense of achievement but they do not see the need of salvation.	2% Christian. Anglican and Methodist contact.	n/a
O4	About 65 members of an Elderly Citizens Group (Over 60s), mainly women, meeting weekly. Mostly widows; a few work.	Social class IV. In need of friendship.	25% Christian. They meet on Baptist premises. The minister and various members are in contact.	Mr D G Collins 18 Broad Park Road Peverell Plymouth PL3 4PX
O5	About 100 members of a Bowling Club at Bideford, meeting weekly. Middle-aged and retired. Most are professional or self-employed.	Social class I, II & III. Sometimes attend a special service, otherwise apathetic.	10% Christian. Anglican, Baptist, Methodist and URC are in contact.	n/a
O6	About 25 men and women meeting in Dawlish for regular debates. All middle-aged or over.	Social class I, II, III; strong social awareness. Intellectual objections to religion.	10% Christian. Anglican and Baptist churches in the area. Two members try to introduce Christian subjects.	Rev Ian Burley Highcroft Backeridge Road Teignmouth Devon TQ14 8NX
O7	A group of about 30 young men and women interested in folk music and based in Plymouth — mostly clerical workers or students, and mainly younger age groups.	Social class III. Their main concerns are money and relationships. There is a lack of Christian contact.	2% Christian. Anglican and Baptist churches in the area.	Rev J Evans Mutley Baptist Church Haindiscombe Road Mutley Plymouth PL4

Description & Location	Characteristics	Openings for Outreach	Contact Person
O8 About 50 housewives over 60 years old belonging to a Women's Institute at Croyde.	Social class I & II. Living in a very prosperous area they have no specific needs. They see no need to go to church.	Negligible number of Christians. There is contact with the Baptists and Anglicans and a Roman Catholic Summer Church.	n/a
O9 About 25 members of a caring group attached to a medical practice in Paignton. Various ages, men and women.	Social class I, II & III. Aware of social needs; may feel that community service is more useful than religious faith.	30% Christian. Baptist and Anglican contact.	n/a

Total population:	605,000
Estimated number attending church:	69,000
Total number not regularly attending church:	**536,000**
Non-attenders as percentage of population:	89%

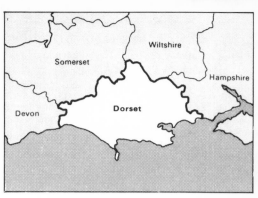

Number of people not regularly attending church:

Age		Sex	
Under 15:	96,000	**Men:**	252,000
15-19:	37,000	**Women:**	284,000
20-29:	75,000		
30-44:	86,000		
45-64:	129,000		
65 or over:	113,000		

SOCIAL/COMMUNITY GROUPS

	Description & Location	Characteristics	Openings for Outreach	Contact Person
S1	About 8,000 low earners living on a 1950s council estate in Bournemouth, all rented accommodation. Some retired. Unskilled work, some 'moonlighting' as domestics in hotels.	Social class V and unemployed. Need friendship, support, job opportunities. Christianity is seen as 'middle class' and irrelevant.	1% Christian. Anglican and Baptist contact.	Rev J R Moore The Rectory 51 Millhams Road Bournemouth BH10 7LJ
S2	A group of about 450 unemployed living in 'bed-sits' in Bournemouth. Unskilled men and women of mixed ages.	Social class V and unemployed. Need job opportunities.	1% Christian. Two unemployed men are undertaking outreach.	Rev R V Fidge 51 Watcombe Road Southbourne Bournemouth Dorset BH6 3LU
S3	About 350 men living in mainly new housing at Wimborne. Work for B.A.C. in offices, computing etc.	Social class II and III. No sense of need for faith or church.	No known Christians in the group. There is a local Anglican church.	n/a
S4	Large numbers living in Bournemouth engaged in secretarial, management or professional work. Men and women, all ages.	Social class I, II and III. Not concerned with any spiritual needs but with materialism and self-sufficiency.	The number of Christians is not known. Anglican and Baptist contact.	Rev Alan Fisher, JP 54 Durrington Road Boscombe East Bournemouth BH7 6QB
S5	About 10,000 living on private estates in old villages around Wimborne. Mostly young families. Employed as teachers, or in independent business or managerial.	Social class I, II and III. The group have very few needs. Many have bad memories of Sunday School or RE at day school.	5% Christian. There are evangelical teams and door-to-door visiting.	Rev Paul Harris The Manse Newtown Lane Corfe Mullen Wimborne Dorset BH21 3EY

DORSET

	Description & Location	Characteristics	Openings for Outreach	Contact Person
O1	12 young people at Christchurch, employed as shop assistants, factory or garage workers. Men and women.	Social class III, IV and V. They meet for friendship. Concerned about money, relationships, etc. Many feel that churches are hypocritical.	Number of Christians not known. Baptist, URC and Anglican churches in area.	Mr Peter Ali Moorlands Bible College Christchurch Dorset BH23 7AT
O2	Large numbers of holiday-makers at Southbourne. All ages, their occupations not known. Seasonal visitors.	They have no time for the Gospel.	There is a need for services and ministry for the believers. Baptist contact.	Rev R V Fidge 51 Watcombe Road Southbourne Bournemouth Dorset BH6 3LU

Total population:	608,000
Estimated number attending church:	51,000
Total number not regularly attending church:	**557,000**
Non-attenders as percentage of population:	92%

Number of people not regularly attending church:

Age		Sex	
Under 15:	122,000	**Men:**	273,000
15-19:	45,000	**Women:**	284,000
20-29:	78,000		
30-44:	106,000		
45-64:	128,000		
65 or over:	78,000		

SOCIAL/COMMUNITY GROUPS

	Description & Location	Characteristics	Openings for Outreach	Contact Person
S1	A group of 50 retired men and women who meet at the Community Centre, Kelloe, Durham	Social class V. All elderly unskilled. In need of friendship. Strong sense of community and suspicion of anything different.	30% Christian. Anglican and Methodist contact. The group is run by a member of the Parish Church.	Rev R Stapleton The Vicarage Kelloe Co Durham DH6 4PT
S2	About 30,000 people living on a 30-year-old estate at Peterlee which is still growing. It is built where many pits were closed. All are miners or unemployed. Many retired.	Social class III and IV. Their main concern is lack of money and work. Their attitude to religion is indifference, apathy and boredom.	10% Christian. There is great co-operation between the churches. RC, Anglican, Methodist and the Peterlee Christian Mission.	Rev A Lawson Methodist Manse Bede Way Town Centre Peterlee Co Durham SR8 1AD
S3	1,500 unemployed at Shildon, a large number of men in their teens or 20s. Semi-skilled who would have worked in local factories.	Social class IV. They have a conscious need for work and to be creative. They need a purpose in life. They consider that society and the church sees them as useless.	10% Christian. Anglican contact. There are inter-church plans for a full-time worker.	Rev V Ashwin St John's Vicarage Shildon Co Durham DL4 1DW

OCCASIONAL GROUPS

O1	About 200 men and women belonging to a Working Men's Club and Railway Institute in Shildon. All work in railway engineering. Various ages, meeting for drink and friendship.	Social classes III, IV and V. Concerned about growing unemployment.	5% Christian. All call themselves Anglican and the local church has contact.	n/a

	Description & Location	Characteristics	Openings for Outreach	Contact Person
O2	Members of Working Men's Clubs living on estates around Consett. Mainly men of all ages, many young, manual workers in heavy industry.	Social class IV and V. Concerned about unemployment. Church is seen as irrelevant or 'for women', but some men most open to Gospel because material world is letting them down.	4% Christian. RC have greatest contact. Some Christian youth workers active.	Rev M Staton 10 West View Blackhill Consett Co Durham DH8 0HJ

Total population:	671,000
Estimated number attending church:	77,000
Total number not regularly attending church:	**594,000**
Non-attenders as percentage of population:	89%

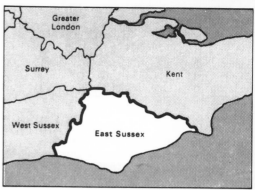

Number of people not regularly attending church:

Age		Sex	
Under 15:	101,000	**Men:**	273,000
15-19:	47,000	**Women:**	321,000
20-29:	83,000		
30-44:	101,000		
45-64:	137,000		
65 or over:	125,000		

SOCIAL/COMMUNITY GROUPS

	Description & Location	Characteristics	Openings for Outreach	Contact Person
S1	About 2,000 people, mainly married with families, living on huge estates, both council and private, at Eastbourne. Mostly young or middle-aged, working in factories, offices, hotels and shops.	Mainly non manual social class III. Problems connected with marriage and loneliness. Local churches do not seem to relate to their needs.	Less than 1% Christian. There are Free Evangelical Church house meetings, and the Church of England also have contact.	n/a
S2	A group of 1,000 lower-income people living on council or housing association dwellings on two estates at Mayfield. Employment is in agriculture, and there are large numbers of young people.	Social groups III & IV. Concern is for adequate employment, housing and education. Mutual cultural alienation divides them from the Church. Part of the group is just not interested.	2 to 3% Christian. There are Anglican and Roman Catholic churches in contact, and some mission work proposed.	Mr C Silver 10 Rothermead Mayfield East Sussex TN20 6EG
S3	2,000 people living on a council estate at Crowborough. Employed as council workers, tradesmen etc. Normal age range.	Social groups IV & V. Their main need is to improve their standard of living. There is a cultural prejudice towards the Gospel.	3% Christian. The Church of England is in contact. A full-time worker has been appointed.	Rev P J Lenon The Vicarage Crowborough East Sussex HN6 1ED
S4	2,000 followers of the teachings of Rudolph Steiner at Forest Row. Many are employed in supplying a wide range of services to the group. There are many young people in the Steiner educational establishments.	Social groups I & II. Many call themselves Christians and some occasionally attend church services. They consider their anthroposophical interpretation of Christianity, including a brief in reincarnation, is superior to normal Christian belief.	A few Christians try to bridge the gap. Those who go to church attend Anglican services.	n/a

S5 Old people living at Alfriston, who meet at funerals and at the crematorium. None are now working. Men and women.

Social groups I & II. All are old and frightened. They are past caring about the Gospel.

45% are Christians. The others are long past outreach. Anglicans and URC have most contact.

n/a

OCCASIONAL GROUPS

O1 Large numbers of young people in Hastings who are addicted to hard line drugs. They live in down-town bed sits and basements etc. They usually live on social security, but some do casual work. Ages 15-30 and both sexes.

Social groups IV & V. They need help with the underlying causes of their drug problem. They are very conscious of being dropouts and 'hooked' on drugs.

One known Christian. Individual members of the Baptist church undertake outreach, and the Elim church is also in contact.

Mr J Webster
27 Clinton Crescent
St Leonards-on-Sea
Sussex
TN38 0RN

Total population: 1,484,000

Estimated number
attending church: 122,000

**Total number not regularly
attending church: 1,362,000**

Non-attenders as
percentage of population: 92%

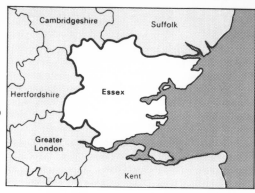

Number of people not regularly attending church:

Age		Sex	
Under 15:	313,000	**Men:**	667,000
15-19:	109,000	**Women:**	695,000
20-29:	191,000		
30-44:	272,000		
45-64:	300,000		
65 or over:	177,000		

SOCIAL/COMMUNITY GROUPS

	Description & Location	Characteristics	Openings for Outreach	Contact Person
S1	People living on a post-war housing development at Chelmsford. Most are under 45 years old. Men and women. Most employed in technology and commerce.	Social classes I, II & III. Many with higher education. They enjoy a good standard of living. They live in an aggressive and competitive society, and know little of Christianity or Christians.	5% Christian. The Anglican and Baptist churches are in contact.	Mr C R Norrish 12 Beach's Drive Chelmsford Essex CM1 2NJ
S2	About 20,000 residents of Basildon New Town. All ages. Men and women. Employed in light industry factories.	Social groups III, IV & V. Many originated from East London and have a common cultural background. Their background is traditionally anti-Church, and there is little sense of spiritual need. There is widespread marital iregularity.	1% Christian. The Anglican, Roman Catholic and Baptist churches are in contact. There is visitation, magazine distribution and publicity in local press.	Rev D Leigh Williams St Andrews Vicarage 3 The Fremnells Basildon Essex SS14 2QX
S3	Gypsies who live on two permanent sites in Harlow. They are caravan dwellers and there are the usual facilities on the sites. There are a large number of young people. Men and women. The main occupations are painting and decorating and scrap iron. Some are also involved in fruit picking.	Social class V, unskilled. There are financial problems, as well as alcohol abuse, violence and illiteracy. This last problem, as well as superstitious religious beliefs, is a block to their knowing the Gospel.	Number of Christians not known. There is a local Elim Pentecostal church in regular contact with the Christians on the sites, and they have held evangelistic meetings.	Mr W R B Robb 19 Longbanks Harlow Essex CM18 7NT

Description & Location	Characteristics	Openings for Outreach	Contact Person
S4 A street in Chelmsford on a private housing estate with 50 inhabitants. Mainly families with parents in 30s or 40s and children at school. Employed in teaching, accountancy and electronics.	Social groups I, II & III. All maintain a high standard of living. Main blocks to the Good News are lack of consciousness of sin and their image of the denominations.	8% Christian. The Church of England and the Brethren are in contact.	Mr M Hall 16 Barrington Close Gt Baddow Chelmsford Essex CM2 7AX
S5 People living in high rise and low rise council flats near Barking. About 7,500 persons, of all ages. Men and women. Engaged in production line work and building.	Social group IV. They are in general alienated from the Church and their attitude is one of ignorance and apathy.	Number of Christians very small, about ½%. The Anglican, Evangelical Free Church and Elim have all completed door-to-door evangelism	Rev R S Williams 12 Thorpe Road Barking Essex IG11 9XJ
S6 A group of about 1,500 persons from 500 homes on a bungalow estate at Ilford. Includes a lot of retired people. Men and women. Many running own businesses or in lower management.	Social group II. Most have progressed from inner city to suburbs, as they have advanced financially. Main block to the Gospel is complacency.	5% Christian. Anglican church and Christian Brethren are in contact. The latter have occasional door-to-door visitation.	Mr E Skinner 20 Morrab Gdns Seven Kings Ilford Essex IG3 9HL
S7 Some 5,000 to 12,000 residents of very large council estates at Harlow. High density housing with restricted amenities. Mainly under 50. Men and women. Employed in a wide range of light and service industries.	Social group IV. An intensely secular, materialistic environment. There is working class prejudice against organised religion, and there has been saturation by Jehovah's Witnesses and sects.	1% Christian. The Church of England have contact and arrange visitation, house groups and regular large scale evangelistic missions. Roman Catholic church also has contact.	Canon Donald Knight The Rectory 43 Upper Park Harlow Essex CM20 1TW
S8 500 of all ages living on several council estates at Harlow.	Social group IV. They are connected by their neighbourhood and the school. A proportion are frightened at the way the world is going. Ignorance and a false stereotyped image of the Church keep them from the Gospel.	2% Christian. Contact through the local parish church and the Baptists.	Mr R F H Howarth 5 Staffords Harlow Essex CM17 0JR
S9 50,000 on large estate at Dagenham. Working on car production or in pharmaceuticals. A lot of young people. Men and women.	Social groups III & IV. Main concerns are job security and health. They are complacent and mainly concerned with maintaining their increasing affluence.	½% Christian. The Church of England, the Methodists and Roman Catholics are in the area, and some outreach has been attempted.	Rev D E Spratley Dagenham Vicarage 86 Rogers Road Dagenham Essex RT10 8JX

Description & Location	Characteristics	Openings for Outreach	Contact Person
S10 Some 400 men and women in the village of Thorpe le Soken. Some have retired from town and city areas. Others commute to work.	Mainly social class III. Non-manual. Little sense of need.	Some Christians in the group.	n/a
Three groups at Epping			
S11 Group 1 2,000 London overspill estate. All ages. Men and women.	The first and second groups are mainly of skilled and semi-skilled workers. Worldly with no spiritual experience.	5% Christian, a few in each group. Apart from the activities of the town churches there is no outreach.	n/a
S12 Group 2 1,000 living on a council estate. All ages. Men and women.			
S13 Group 3 A private estate of 1,000 people. All ages. Men and women.	Social group I, living in town houses. Concerned with materialism and too busy for God.		n/a
S14 Between 50 and 80 retired people living by the sea at East Clacton. Men and women who had worked in offices in London before retirement.	Social group III. Mainly concerned with the problems of old age. Materialistic and indifferent to the Gospel.	10% Christian. The Baptists, Methodists and Church of England have contact.	Rev P Chevill 87 Fleetwood Ave Holland-on-Sea Clacton Essex CO15 5RX

ETHNIC/LINGUISTIC GROUPS

Description & Location	Characteristics	Openings for Outreach	Contact Person
E1 Asians who have moved into Ilford since 1970. Hindus, Sikhs and Muslims from various countries. Most of them work in shops. Men and women of all ages.	They are from various countries and speak various languages. They want to get on financially. Main blocks are cultural differences and lack of contact with Christians.	No known outreach.	Mr E Skinner Morrab Gardens Seven Kings Ilford Essex IG3 9HL

OCCASIONAL GROUPS

Description & Location	Characteristics	Openings for Outreach	Contact Person
O1 200 members of a PTA at Rayne. Mostly young parents aged 20-30, working as sales representatives, on the shop floor or in clerical work.	Social groups III & IV. Concerned with children and general family welfare. Unwilling to be committed to any point of view or any regular activity beyond the family. Materialism a major block.	4% Christian. Sunday School and baptism contacts with the Church of England.	Rev M Sellix The Rectory Shalford Road Rayne Braintree Essex CM7 5BT

	Description & Location	Characteristics	Openings for Outreach	Contact Person
O2	Lions charity and fund raising social group at Braintree. 150 members, middle aged adults. Men and women working as company directors, secretaries, teachers or self employed. They meet monthly.	Social groups II & III. Mainly conscious of material things and general family welfare. They have the idea that good works accrue virtue and that the Church is a similar though irrelevant organization.	1% Christian. There are churches in the area and there is pastoral visitation. Might be reached by social events with speakers, or by joining them in charity projects.	Rev M Sellix The Rectory Shalford Braintree Essex CM7 5BT
O3	A group of between 50 and 200 motor cyclists based at Barkingside. Young people of both sexes. Many unemployed. Others in a variety of jobs.	Social groups IV & V. They lack all consciousness of sin. Work is their most pressing need. Their whole way of life is lawless, undisciplined and oblivious of the Gospel.	1% Christian. Baptist and Pentecostalist churches in contact. There are three young men involved in outreach among the group. Might be approached through music, videos etc.	Mr Matthew Clarke 6 Rise Park Boulevard Romford Essex RM1 4PP
O4	Families involved in summer sailing activities on the River Crouch. About 1,500 people, younger families, mostly professional and often London based	Social groups II & III. They have no time for anything apart from their work and sailing.	1% Christian. The denominations represented are Anglican, URC and Baptist. Might be reached by special evangelistic work, perhaps by fellow sailing enthusiasts.	Rev M L Ellis 13 Glebe Way Burnham-on-Crouch Essex CM0 8QJ
O5	A Rotary Club and Inner Wheel. 60 business men and women in commerce, banking or the professions. All are middle aged.	Social group II. Very conscious of community service for others and their own business pressures.	20% Christian. The Church of England, Methodists and the Baptists all have contact.	n/a
O6	About 80 members of sport and social clubs and others with sporting links in Enfield. Young to middle aged. Mainly men but women supporters. Variety of occupations.	All social groups. Not conscious of any spiritual needs.	4% Christian. Church of England has contact.	n/a

GLOUCESTERSHIRE

Total population: 506,000

Estimated number
attending church: 53,000

**Total number not regularly
attending church: 453,000**

Non-attenders as
percentage of population: 90%

Number of people not regularly attending church:

Age		Sex	
Under 15:	104,000	**Men:**	222,000
15-19:	36,000	**Women:**	231,000
20-29:	63,000		
30-44:	82,000		
45-64:	100,000		
65 or over:	68,000		

SOCIAL/COMMUNITY GROUPS

	Description & Location	Characteristics	Openings for Outreach	Contact Person
S1	500 people on a housing estate at Bredon. Married couples with young children working on computer programming, selling, teaching, personnel management. Adults mainly in early 30s and young children.	Social classes I & II. They have a need for something more secure than material prosperity. Ignorance keeps them from the Gospel.	5% Christian. The Anglican parish church has connections and there are other free church groups undertaking outreach.	Rev C J Ridout The Rectory Bredon Tewkesbury Gloucester GL20 7LF

ETHNIC/LINGUISTIC GROUPS

E1	About 9,000 immigrants in the city of Gloucester. They include West Indians, Indians, a few Pakistanis and Ukrainians. Some have unskilled work, some are in the professions and some unemployed. There are many young people.	Most of the Asians are Moslems and 57% of them read English. The languages are English, Ukrainian and the languages of the Indian sub continent. Difficulty in social contact with Christians outside their communities.	Most of the West Indians and Central Europeans are nominally Christian. 1% of the Asians are. At present there is a special project of outreach.	Capt A J Fitch 36 Howard Street Gloucester GL1 4US

GREATER LONDON

Total population:	6,765,000
Estimated number attending church:	559,000
Total number not regularly attending church:	**6,206,000**
Non-attenders as percentage of population:	92%

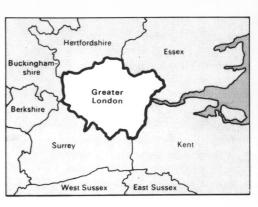

Number of people not regularly attending church:

Age		Sex	
Under 15:	1,071,000	**Men:**	3,018,000
15-19:	497,000	**Women:**	3,188,000
20-29:	830,000		
30-44:	1,303,000		
45-64:	1,489,000		
65 or over:	1,016,000		

SOCIAL/COMMUNITY GROUPS

	Description & Location	Characteristics	Openings for Outreach	Contact Person
S1	A group of 1,000 commuters living around Hanwell. Men and women of all ages, though more young than older people. Most working in offices of all kinds.	Social class III, non-manual. Their main aim is to prosper and leave the area. Their ambitious and materialistic life-style keeps them from the Gospel. They tend to be very independent.	5% Christian. The Roman Catholic Church is in contact through visitation.	n/a
S2	400 people living in the village of Laleham near Staines. Mixed age range of people employed in senior management and the professions.	Social groups I & II. They are comfortably off and have little or no sense of need for the Gospel. They are too busy for God.	10% Christian. The Anglican Parish Church is in contact with pastoral care and a free news letter. They plan a Mission in October 1984.	Rev P R Brown Laleham Vicarage Staines Middlesex TW18 1SB
S3	5,000 council tenants geographically isolated from the Church in Ealing. Men and women of all ages mainly employed in local government and in manual and non-manual work.	Social classes III & IV. Their main concerns are material and emotional. A lack of communication of the Good News impairs their understanding of it.	2% Christian. The Free Churches and the Anglican Parish Church are in contact.	Mrs Joan Porter 31 Maple Grove Ealing London W5 4LA
S4	A community of 1,000 folk on a well planned council estate, the Lennox Estate, at Roehampton. It is situated near to a park and expensive private dwellings. Men and women of all ages employed mostly as builders, tradespeople and engineers.	Social groups III & IV. Many would feel a lack of friendship and lack of order in life. Class division and no 'live' church cut them off from the Gospel although many are open.	1% Christian. The Roman Catholic Church is in contact.	Mr M A Rhodes 55 Newton Avenue Acton London W3 8AS

	Description & Location	Characteristics	Openings for Outreach	Contact Person
S5	7,000 living in the parish of St Augustine's in Highbury. Ordinary people going about their everyday lives. Men and women of all ages.	Mainly social class III, though all classes represented. Their main concerns are for family, jobs and career prospects. To most the Gospel is irrelevant; they feel no need for it.	About 100 Christians. The Church of England, Baptist and Congregational Churches are all engaged in outreach but the impact is small.	Rev A Must St Augustine's Vicarage 108 Highbury New Park London N5 2DR
S6	5,000 people living in high rise flats in South Acton. They include a substantial immigrant minority. Most are employed in factories or manual work. There is average unemployment.	Social class V. Most are conscious of their mundane lives and of loneliness. The main obstacles to accepting the Gospel include discontentment, drink and depression.	0.5% Christian. The Baptist Church and the Church of England are equally involved in outreach. There is a need for cell groups to reach individuals. Old people's clubs and holidays for children are other means of outreach.	Mr M A Rhodes 55 Newton Avenue Acton London W3 8AS
S7	200 elderly men and women living in council accommodation in W1.	Social classes IV & V. They are characterised by their apathy and self-sufficiency.	2% Christian. The Anglican, Methodist and Roman Catholic Churches are in contact.	n/a
S8	About 200 homeless people in the parish of Waterloo in Central London. Mostly unemployed older men.	Social class V. Often with psychiatric or alcohol problems. They have basic physical needs: shelter, clothing, food and heating. They associate the Church with the society which has rejected them.	The Salvation Army and the London Embankment Mission in contact. The crypt of the parish church at Waterloo is to be turned into a day centre for this group.	n/a
S9	Many thousands of upper and middle class people living in their own houses in West Dulwich. Many commute to the City. They are employed in a wide range of professions. Men and women of all ages.	Social classes I, II & III. They do not appear to have any conscious needs. Their chief concerns are to do with material prosperity.	The number of Christians is not known. There is no known outreach. The Anglican and Roman Catholic Churches are in the area.	Mr A McKie 27 Lovelace Road London SE21 8JY
S10	15,000 young people aged 11 to 18. They attend some 30 different schools in the Waltham Forest area. Many are heading for unemployment.	Social class V. They are mainly concerned about the future and about a job. Spiritual oppression in the area and lack of Church involvement keep them from the Gospel.	3% Christian. Outreach through Waltham Youth for Christ. There are Anglican churches in the area.	Mr Pete Gilbert 3 Abbott's Park Road Leyton London E10 6HT

Description & Location	Characteristics	Openings for Outreach	Contact Person
S11 A large number of unemployed men in the Canning Town area. Male unemployment locally is around 50%. There is some crime and much moonlighting.	Social classes III & IV. Employment and financial worries are great. Evangelism appears to be out of context.	Very very few Christians. The Anglican and Roman Catholic Churches have limited contact. The Mayflower Centre is active.	n/a
S12 Thousands of young people, professionals and graduates, who have moved to London to start careers in accountancy and banking.	Social class I & II. They need to establish friendships in their new areas. Studying for exams and the stress of starting a career leave little time for the Gospel.	5-10% Christian. There are lunch-time services at churches in the City.	Mr David Buchan Wayside Sweet Lane Peaslake Guildford Surrey GU5 9SH
S13 The women in Canning Town. Many are married and almost all are attached to a partner so that their lives tend to revolve around their men. Some have factory work but most are housewives.	Social classes III, IV & V. Their concerns are money, relief from boredom and a need for independence.	Few Christians. The Anglican and Roman Catholic Churches are in contact. The Mayflower Family Centre is active. Mums & Toddlers groups are a means of outreach.	n/a
S14 A small group of 25 neighbours in Catford. Social workers, some police, a nurse and office workers. Several elderly people.	Social classes I, II & III. Their main concerns appear to be financial. Completely indifferent to the Gospel. They use Sundays to catch up at home.	20% Christians. Door-to-door visitation by a local Chapel. There is also an Anglican Church in the area.	Mrs B Armistead Noryl 80 Longhill Road Catford London SE6 1VA
S15 20,000 living in Plumstead. A multi-racial, multi-cultural and multi-faith group. Most are employed in a wide variety of jobs, some in offices in Central London.	All social classes. Ethnic minorities need to be seen to be welcomed by all. Christians need to be aware of the special social needs in Plumstead. Christians are apathetic, treating the Christian faith as an extra for those who want it.	10% Christian. The Methodists, Salvation Army, Baptists, FIEC, Anglicans and Roman Catholics are all in contact. There is door-to-door visitation, house groups, and tract and gospel distribution.	Rev J T Lawson 14 Tuscan Road Plumstead London SE18 1SY
S16 5,500 people in the parish of St Luke's in Hackney. Mixed races and backgrounds linked by deprivation and unemployment. Those employed tend to work in factories or for the local authority.	Social classes IV & V. Main concerns are unemployment, bad housing, coping with alcoholism and violence. They need one-to-one care at a spiritual and social level.	2% Christian. The Anglicans, Pentecostals and Baptists all have contact.	Rev B Snelling St Luke's Vicarage 22 Cassland Road Hackney London E9 7AL

ETHNIC/LINGUISTIC GROUPS

	Description & Location	Characteristics	Openings for Outreach	Contact Person
E1	A group of 150 Ramgaria Sikhs who meet twice a week for worship in their temple at Forest Gate. Originally from India, they work mostly in shops and in the building trade. Mainly older and middle-aged folk.	About 70% read English. Their mother tongue is Punjabi; their religion, Sikh. Their needs are for English language teaching and more social and cultural activities for their leisure time.	There is evangelistic outreach and door-to-door visitation.	Mr Eric Sarfraz Flat 5 69B Station Road Forest Gate London E7 0EU
E2	Many thousands of West Indians settled in West Norwood. Employed mainly as manual labourers or in transport or hospitals.	95% read English which is their mother tongue. Their religion is Christian. Economic pressures and the image of the typical church keep them from the Gospel	25% Christian. There is door-to-door visitation.	Mr Andrew McKie 27 Lovelace Road London SE21 8JY
E3	50 patients at the Sarah Tankel Home for sick Jews at Highbury Grove. They come from various countries.	English is their mother tongue and their religion Judaism. The need of all is medical. Blindness of heart keeps them from the Gospel.	Outreach and service is through nursing.	n/a
E4	Some 12 or more families of Vietnamese boat people on the Ferrier Housing estate at Kidbrooke. Mainly employed as porters and watchmen; others are unemployed.	20% read English. Their first languages are Vietnamese and French. Their religion is either Roman Catholic or Buddhist. They want to learn English and be accepted. There are linguistic and cultural barriers to the Gospel. Racism and their experiences as refugees also cut them off from the Good News.	50% Christian. A words-only, culturally based Christianity serves no purpose. They would be attracted to a loving, caring community.	n/a
E5	Wealthy Arabs in London's West End. They have lived in the area since the early 1970's. It is a mobile community, coming from the Middle East. There is a noticeable number of Kuwaitis.	Their mother tongue is Arabic; their religion, Islam. Their wealth, culture and religion keep them from the Gospel.	No Christian outreach.	n/a
E6	60% of the population of a council estate at New Cross, Deptford. They come from various countries in the West Indies. Very few old people; many children. Unemployment is high; some work in various unskilled jobs.	All can read English which is their mother tongue. Their religion tends to be a sort of 'folk-Christianity'. They are concerned about bad housing, unemployment and domestic tensions. The Gospel is not expressed in terms they can understand.	Less than 5% Christian. Shaftesbury Project doing general evangelism. There is a small Afro-Caribbean church in the area.	Rev Kim Hitch St James's Vicarage St James's London SE14 6AD

Description & Location	Characteristics	Openings for Outreach	Contact Person
E7 Several thousands of Asian immigrants mainly from India, living in terraced housing in Plumstead. They work in supermarkets, shops and the clothing trade. Some are unemployed.	Perhaps some 25% read English easily. Their mother tongue is mainly Hindi. They are conscious of the need for a better standard of living. There is ignorance of the Gospel and cultural differences would be a barrier to receiving the Good News.	No known Christians. There are three Evangelical churches in the area.	Mr K J Newell 100 Cumberland Avenue Welling Kent DA16 2PU
E8 Many thousands of Indians living in Wembley. They are originally from India and Uganda. Mainly employed as shop keepers or wholesalers. The group has lived in the area for some 10 years.	75% can read English; mainly the adult men and the young people. Their mother tongue is mainly Gujerati, and for some, Hindi and Punjabi. The religion of the majority is Hindu. There are some Sikhs, Muslims and Buddhists. There is a great need for acceptance, security and belonging.	Very few Christians. There is door-to-door visitation from time to time. Also work among women and youth work.	Rev Ian Ring 155 Ealing Road Wembley Middlesex HA0 4BY
E9 35,000 Gujeratis settled in Wembley and Brent. Many left Kenya and Uganda in 1968-1972. Shopkeepers and professionals, clerical workers and factory workers. Large numbers of children and young people.	Perhaps 60% read English easily. Their mother tongue is Gujerati and their religion, Hindu. They are very self-sufficient and have their own culture. Pressures to conform make accepting the Gospel difficult.	Very low number of Christians. There is scope for more people to give time, friendship and understanding.	Mr John Root 34 Stanley Avenue Alperton Middlesex HA0 4SB
E10 30,000 people in Central Southall; largely Sikh, Hindu, English and Muslim too. About 30% under the age of 15. Most of those employed are in unskilled jobs.	50% read English easily. The needs the group is most conscious of are the generation gap, fear and a need to integrate. Tradition and a lack of witness cut them off from the Gospel, though they are generally open to it.	About 5% are Christian. There is a Pentecostal, an evangelical Anglican and a Roman Catholic church all undertaking outreach.	Mr M A Rhodes 55 Newton Avenue Acton London W3 8AS
E11 An Asian group mainly from East Africa, but some from the Indian sub-continent, settled in Clapton and Stoke Newington. About 120 people of all ages divided into 30 families. There are many young people. Most of those employed are in the clothing trade and in shop keeping.	25% of the adults and 60% of the children read English. Their mother tongue is Gujerati and their religion Muslim. The main needs are security in the UK and full opportunities for their children. Muslim culture and lack of contact with Christians are barriers to the Good News.	No known Christians and no known outreach.	n/a

Description & Location	Characteristics	Openings for Outreach	Contact Person
E12 A community of some 700 Jewish people living in their own houses in Stanmore. Their occupations are business and professional.	All read English which is their mother tongue. Many would have a knowledge of Hebrew. Their religion is Judaism. Their cultural and religious background keep them from the Gospel.	1% Christian. There is door-to-door visitation. The Christian societies working among the Jews are active.	Rev G D Walker 77 Belmont Lane Stanmore Middlesex HA7 2QA
E13 Some 250 folk from India and East Africa living in Hanwell; some 75 Sikhs, 75 Hindus and 100 Muslims. Most work in shops. There is a wide age range.	50% would read English easily. The mother tongues are Punjabi, Hindi and Urdu. All are conscious of the need for acceptance security. Their culture and tradition keep them from the Gospel.	2% are Christian. There is outreach in the form of fellowship from the local church.	n/a

OCCASIONAL GROUPS

Description & Location	Characteristics	Openings for Outreach	Contact Person
O1 75-100 parents of children attending a private school in Chiswick. They are young to middle aged. Employed in the Civil Service, banking, management or their own businesses.	Their main conscious needs are social and material. Liberal theology, nominal Christianity and self-reliance keep them from the Gospel.	1 to 2% Christian. The Anglican Church is in contact.	Rev W Moody The Manse 51 Wavenden Ave Chiswick London W4 4NT
O2 A group of 1,000 mostly young people living in bed-sits in North London. Various occupations.	Social group III. Many are lonely and very conscious of the need for company.	Number of Christians not known, but there are some. There is a need for house groups to bring Christians together and provide a platform for outreach.	n/a
O3 40 young people in a Youth Club at Forest Gate. All still at school.	They are primarily concerned about getting work. They are apathetic about religion.	10% Christian. Youth Club leaders undertake outreach.	Mr Simon Law 236 Sebert Road Forest Gate London E7 0NP
O4 About 12 boys aged 14 or 15. All from working-class backgrounds.	Social class III, IV & V. Seeking excitement, fun and acceptance. They see Christianity as irrelevant and Christians as having different attitudes and class from them.	No known Christians. The Mayflower Youth Club is the main Christian contact.	Mr Geoff Flynn Mayflower Youth Club Vincent Street London E16 1LZ
O5 65,000 middle-class office workers who live in the suburbs and work each day in and around the Waterloo area. All office workers in managerial, secretarial and clerical posts.	Social classes II & III. Their main concerns are material. They are absorbed in a search for success and Christianity seems irrelevant.	5% Christian. There are lunch-time services in some local churches. Some of the larger companies have Christian fellowships.	n/a

Description & Location	Characteristics	Openings for Outreach	Contact Person
O6 A group of 20 unemployed people in Pinner who meet to share mutual concerns. They are mostly aged 50 and over.	Social group II. In an affluent community, they tend to be concerned with economics. They have a great desire to be needed in society.	There is one Christian in the group who gives pastoral leadership. There are local Anglican and Methodist churches.	Rev D Sampson 68 Love Lane Pinner Middlesex HA5 2EX
O7 About 100 young 'singles'; nurses, students, civil servants, trained solicitors and accountants living in bed-sits, flats and nursing homes in W1.	Social class II & III. They lead busy social lives and tend to be concerned with their jobs. Their main aims are success and to find a partner in life. Many of them are open to hearing the Gospel.	About 5% Christian. The local Church of England is in contact and looking for ideas for innovative outreach.	n/a
O8 100,000 University, college and nursing students living in hostels, rooms and flats in Central London. Men and women aged 18 to 22 years. Future work will be varied but all potentially middle class.	Social class I, II & III. They are conscious of working out their philosophical framework and of a need to establish relationships.	10% Christian. Various chaplaincy churches are in touch. Strong teaching with intellectual content, young people's participating and an emphasis on fellowship are all needed if a church is to reach them.	Mr Alan Rogers Church Secretary The City Temple London EC1A 2DE
O9 6-10 members of an activity group (not a youth club) aged 14 to 20 in the poorer part of Newham. Some are working in labouring and clerical work.	Social classes III, IV & V. Their basic needs are food, security and sex. The Church seems irrelevant to their situation. They lack a knowledge of the Gospel.	A connection with the Mayflower Youth Club, which still keeps in touch with individuals.	Mr & Mrs D & C Seamark 44 Vincent Street Canning Town London E16 1LS
O10 500 single homeless men at Carrington House in Deptford. Most are middle aged but the number of younger ones is increasing. All are unemployed.	Social class unknown. Apart from their material needs, they need a sense of purpose, self-worth and love. There is an absence of close relationships, and a suspicion of the establishment in the Church.	Number of Christians not known. A Roman Catholic priest and the Chaplain to Carrington House work among them.	Rev K Hitch St James's Vicarage St James's London SE14 6AD
O11 30 young mothers and nannies who meet for companionship once a week during school term. Husbands work as pharmacists, company directors and teachers.	Social classes I & II. They are affluent and lack Christian friendship.	15% Christians. The group is led by Christians who plan social and discussion evenings inviting husbands and boyfriends.	Mrs Sue Pierson 48 Peterborough Road London SW6 3EB
O12 150 students at Lee Abbey International Students Hostel in London W8.	All students from various countries and mostly nominally Christian. Their main concerns are financial. Western culture and a cluttered Christianity are the main blocks to them receiving the Gospel.	50% Christian. The hostel is run by a Christian community who offer friendship and share the Gospel with them.	Mrs S Battison Lee Abbey International Students Hostel 57/67 Lexham Gardens London W8 6JJ

Description & Location	Characteristics	Openings for Outreach	Contact Person
O13 100 members of Coldfall Residents Association at Muswell Hill. Men and women in various kinds of employment.	Social groups III, IV & V. Their main concerns are to do with family matters. There is a need for pastoral and social services.	10% Christian. The Christian Brethren and the Church of England are in contact.	Mr J E Small 46 Lauderdale Road East Finchley London N2 9NU
O14 The 25 professional footballers at Crystal Palace, Selhurst Park. All men under 35.	Social class III. They have a need for emotional security. Affluence and hero worship keep them from the Gospel.	5% Christian. They have a Club Chaplain who ministers to them. Individual witness through hospitality is helpful.	Rev N Sands Wickham Rectory Newbury Berks RG16 8HD
O15 150 parents who send their children to Sunday School and Youth Fellowship but who do not attend themselves except on special occasions.	Social group II. They feel no personal spiritual needs. They do not see the relevance of Jesus Christ.	Number of Christians not known. There is outreach.	Mr L F Reveley 25 The Avenue Pinner Middlesex HA5 4BH

GREATER MANCHESTER

Total population: 2,605,000

Estimated number
attending church: 220,000

**Total number not regularly
attending church: 2,385,000**

Non-attenders as
percentage of population: 92%

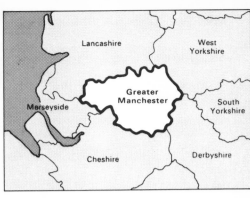

Number of people not regularly attending church:

Age		Sex	
Under 15:	525,000	**Men:**	1,169,000
15-19:	191,000	**Women:**	1,216,000
20-29:	334,000		
30-44:	429,000		
45-64:	572,000		
65 or over:	334,000		

SOCIAL/COMMUNITY GROUPS

	Description & Location	Characteristics	Openings for Outreach	Contact Person
S1	A group of 400 or more men and women living on a council estate at Wigan. Full age range but many over 55. Working in mining, mail order factories, as labourers or at Heinz.	Social group V. They attend the local club for beer and bingo. They worry over unemployment and there is a lack of purpose in their lives. Main block to Gospel is their preconceived ideas of Christianity deriving from childhood, and their 'folk religion'.	10% Christian. The local vicar is undertaking outreach. There is also a Roman Catholic church in the area.	Rev Ian Greenhalgh St Barnabas Vicarage Marsh Green Wigan WN5 0PT
S2	300 to 400 residents of a council estate at Standish. All ages; many are unemployed.	Social group IV. Tied together by the pub and local Labour club. Concerned about work, and think the Church is irrelevant to their needs.	10% Christian. Visitation is undertaken by the Anglicans, Roman Catholics and Methodists.	n/a
S3	The inner city population of Salford. About 98,000 people. Particularly the 28% of the labour force who are unemployed young people aged 16-24. Also the many single parent families and pensioners living alone. Few in these three groups do more than occasional work.	Social groups IV & V. All groups are concerned with money and social support. They see no connection between biblical spirituality and their fight for social justice. The language of the Church is middle class and alien.	5% Christian. Pastoral work, mainly by the Roman Catholics.	Mr K J Argyle 9 Doveleys Road Salford M6 8QW

Description & Location	Characteristics	Openings for Outreach	Contact Person
S4 9,000 houseowners in the parish of Leigh. Many of them are shopkeepers, or skilled artisans. Large numbers of both old and young people.	Social groups I, II & III. Concerned about security of marriage, children's education and health. Materialism is main reason for not knowing the Gospel.	2% Christian. There is an Anglican magazine, house groups, and visitation. The local churches are Anglican, Roman Catholic, Methodist and Free Evangelical.	Rev Norman Wain Pennington Vicarage Schofield Street Leigh Lancs WN7 4HT
S5 Indigenous population living in terraced or council housing in Bolton, 2 miles from the city centre. Various ages and employment.	Semi-skilled workers. Main needs are financial. An area where much religious folklore survives, and the Church is seen as irrelevant.	Number of Christians unknown. There is a Church of England and URC.	Rev J C Melling St Michael's Rectory 355 Green Lane Great Lever Bolton BL3 2LU
S6 1,000 young adults and middle aged people on new housing estates at Droylsden. Mostly engaged in office work or engineering.	Social groups II & III. All are concerned with material wealth, and worry about what others will think.	1% Christian. The Pentecostals work with literature and personal evangelism, and there is also an Anglican church in contact.	Rev Colin Carson 13 Victory Grove Audenshaw Manchester M34 5GH
S7 Between 20,000 and 50,000 men living in working class areas in Bolton. All ages and working in boring and repetitive and non-responsible jobs.	Social groups IV & V. They like to be seen as men. The Church is for women and irrelevant. They think they are too tough to join. Most of the men have 'macho' values but in fact lack courage and responsibility.	Less than 1% Christian. The Church of England and Roman Catholics are in most contact but there is no direct outreach.	Rev R J N Cook 208 Derby Street Bolton BL3 6JN
S8 About 7,000 residents of inner city corporation housing estates at Harpurhey. Their employment is mainly manual and labouring. Large numbers of old and young people.	Social groups IV & V. Problems are financial and their general inability to cope with life. Prejudiced against the Church because of media image and class identity.	1% Christian. The Anglican clergy and keen church members undertake outreach.	Rev Richard Hindley The Rectory 95 Church Lane Harpurhey Manchester M9 1BG

ETHNIC/LINGUISTIC GROUPS

Description & Location	Characteristics	Openings for Outreach	Contact Person
E1 25% of the parish of Great Lever, Bolton are immigrants from Pakistan. They work as taxi drivers, small shop owners or unskilled labourers. Mixed ages, but few elderly. Men and women.	60% read English. The mother tongue is mainly Urdu with a few speaking Gujerati and their religion is Islam. Solidarity with their own culture keeps them from the Gospel.	No Christians. There is a free church Minister leading an evangelical team.	n/a

Description & Location	Characteristics	Openings for Outreach	Contact Person
E2 17,000 to 20,000 Asians at Bolton, mainly in two inner urban areas. A large number of young people. They come from India, Kenya and Uganda. They are employed in textile and clothing manufacture, and as bus drivers etc., but there is high unemployment.	50% speak and read English. Urdu and Gujerati are their mother tongues, and their religions are Islam and Hinduism. The great need is to be accepted as British and to make life successful and worthwhile. Their language and culture and desire to maintain these keep them ignorant of Christianity.	Under 1% Christian. There is an Asian Christian Fellowship meeting quarterly. There are prayer groups, friendship and evangelism.	Rev Richard Cook 208 Derby Street Bolton BL3 6JN
E3 35,000 Jews of various origins in Greater Manchester in several areas of high concentration. They originated mainly in Eastern Europe. Employed in the professions or trading. Mixed ages.	100% English speaking. It is their mother tongue, but some speak a little Yiddish. Their religion is Judaism, but many have no religion. Prejudiced against the Gospel because of centuries of 'Christian' oppression.	Less than 1% Christian. Outreach by CMJ, CWI and TMT	Mr Ron Axtell Deanery Gardens Bury New Road Salford M7 0WT
E4 200 refugees from North and South Vietnam and Cambodia who have settled in the north part of Manchester. Mostly young and employed in labouring or semi-skilled work. Men and women.	30% read English. Their mother tongue is mainly Cantonese and their religion is Buddhism or ancestor worship. Their greatest need is to keep links with their country of origin. Cultural and language barriers to Christianity.	1% Christian. No known outreach.	Rev T S R Chow St Paul's Rectory Erskine Road Blackley Manchester M9 2RB
E5 60 members of a West Indian youth club at Moss Side. All are unemployed, aged from 18-28. Most born here but parents come from Jamaica. Men and women.	80% read English, which is the mother tongue. If any at all their religion is Rastafarian. Their experience of living in a hostile white culture keeps them from Christianity.	No known Christians. There is a student from the Methodist College working among them.	Rev T J Stuckey 53 Alexandra Road South Manchester M16 8GH
E6 4,000 or more Indians and Pakistanis in the Coppice and the Glodwick areas of Oldham. Employed in mainly manual jobs or business. Men and women of all ages.	50% read English. Their mother tongues are Urdu or Gujerati and their religion is Hinduism or Islam. Needs are material and desire to be accepted. Social customs and family ties keep them from the Gospel.	No known Christians and no outreach being undertaken.	Pastor David Johnston Hartford Grange Wellington Road Oldham OL8 4DD

Description & Location	Characteristics	Openings for Outreach	Contact Person
O1 The poor, deprived, lonely and unemployed of the inner city at Moss Side. It is a large group of all ages, though the young stand out on their own. Few employed. Men and women. Meet each day at the 'Drop-In' Centre.	Social group V. They need help to achieve their rights and to handle their finances. They cannot see 'Good News' or love from anyone, and are frightened of Church.	1.2% Christian. Outreach by the Drop-In Centre and practical help from churches using Government CP schemes and Church of England Housing Association. Methodists, Roman Catholics and Baptists also involved.	Mr Terence Young 67 Wilbraham Road Manchester M14 7DN
O2 500 members of Didsbury Civic Society, formed to preserve the living standards of Didsbury. Men and women, mainly in older age group. Meet monthly.	Social groups I & II. Self contained group anxious to maintain a high standard of living. They see the Christian faith in terms of being good citizens.	10% Christian. There are Anglican and Methodist churches in area.	n/a

HAMPSHIRE

Total population: 1,486,000

Estimated number
attending church: 111,000

**Total number not regularly
attending church: 1,375,000**

Non-attenders as
percentage of population: 93%

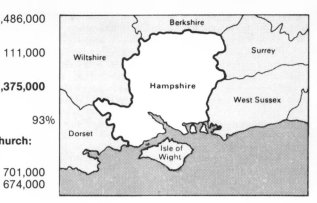

Number of people not regularly attending church:

Age		Sex	
Under 15:	316,000	**Men:**	701,000
15-19:	124,000	**Women:**	674,000
20-29:	220,000		
30-44:	261,000		
45-64:	289,000		
65 or over:	165,000		

SOCIAL/COMMUNITY GROUPS

	Description & Location	Characteristics	Openings for Outreach	Contact Person
S1	A group of about 30 young people live at Aldermoor. Mainly teenage boys with no employment.	Unskilled and unemployed or soon to leave school, with no hope of employment. They lack any understanding of Christianity.	There do not appear to be any Christians, but some attend an open Youth Club at the Anglican church.	Rev C Atkins 1 Tangmere Drive Lords Hill Southampton SO1 8GY
S2	1,250 on a mainly council estate at Overton. All ages, men and women. Many work at local paper mill.	Semi-skilled. Social class IV. Their families have often been living in the village for generations, and this shapes their attitude towards the Church.	Less than 1% Christian. The Anglicans have contact, and there has been some leafletting.	Rev N P Cumming 54 Lordsfield Gdns Overton Basingstoke Hants RG25 3EW
S3	A rural community of 1,500 consisting of people from all walks of life, knit together by living in villages scattered around Romsey. All ages. Men and women. Various employment.	All social groups except the unskilled. There is a tendency to assume that they are Christians, combined with general indifference and apathy towards the Gospel.	6% Christians. Anglican, Baptist and Methodist churches all have contact, but this is very limited.	n/a
S4	500 people living on a council estate at Oakley. All ages represented. Men and women.	Social groups IV & V. There is little binding them together as a community. They would probably feel that they would not 'belong' in a church.	4% Christian. Church of England, Roman Catholics and Methodists all have contacts.	Canon J C Litton The Rectory Rectory Road Oakley Hants RG23 7ED

	Description & Location	Characteristics	Openings for Outreach	Contact Person
S5	Rowner, an area in Gosport where problem families are collected. Many young and old people, both sexes. Various employment including Navy and MOD.	Social groups III, IV & V. There are about 100 children, many of whom are disturbed. Divorce and illegitimacy are common and moral standards seem very low.	Apparently no Christians. A small Gospel Hall endeavours to spread the word of God. Great need for more committed people to work in this area, particularly with the children.	n/a
S6	A council estate at Alton with inhabitants of all ages. Men and women.	Social groups III, IV & V. The church is used only on special occasions. They have a preoccupation with material things. There have been several generations without faith or teaching.	The local Anglican church has attempted visitations with little success.	Canon Robert Eke St Lawrence Vicarage Alton Hants GU34 2BW
S7	A group of young graduates working in administration and research in government or defence-based industry based at Farnborough. Mainly aged 25-35. Both sexes — wives usually working.	Social groups I & II. They are concerned with success and career development, expecting that present material affluence will continue. Many have experienced sophisticated scientific training but virtually no religious education.	1 to 5% Christian. There are informed Christian groups at their places of work and a local Anglican church has contact.	n/a
S8	1,000 people in working class households living on council estates at Liphook. Many work at the Civil Service Stores Depot and local service industries. There are men and women of all ages.	Social groups IV & V. The history of the church in that area has been biased towards the middle class. There is a lack of contact with committed Christians of a similar background.	2% Christians. There is a little contact with the Church of England and the Brethren.	Rev R Ewbank The Rectory 6 Portsmouth Road Liphook Hants GU30 7AA
S9	600 people living in an area of Southampton towards the docks, in old terraced houses. The group includes some Chinese, ex-students, unemployed, drop-outs and prostitutes. Large numbers of young people. Both sexes.	Unskilled, social group V, with a number of unemployed. Fixed patterns of ideas and anti-establishment attitudes very much in evidence.	Very few Christians. The evangelicals and the Pentecostals have contact.	Rev R A Palmer 9 Lyon Street Southampton SO2 0LD

HAMPSHIRE

ETHNIC/LINGUISTIC GROUPS

	Description & Location	Characteristics	Openings for Outreach	Contact Person
E1	A semi-housed community with gypsy origins at Liphook, numbering 250 people. They work in scrap metal or as log merchants. Some work in building and others in the second hand car trade. Countries of origin not known.	50% can read English easily. It is now their mother tongue. Their religion is a vague folk Christianity. They have a sense of alienation from a largely comfortable middle-class Church.	Very few Christians. Anglican clergy in contact for official services.	Rev R Ewbank Liphook Rectory 6 Portsmouth Road Liphook Hants GU30 7AA
E2	2,000 Asians living mainly in terraced houses in the inner city of Southampton. They work on the buses, as builders, shopkeepers and there are many unemployed. Most are from Pakistan. Both sexes, and many children and young people.	70% can read English. They are Sikhs and Hindus. Southampton City Council has assisted racial harmony by supplying buildings and land for social and spiritual purposes. Strong traditional ties are block to receiving Good News.	About 5% are Christians. There is no known outreach.	Rev Richard Palmer 9 Lyon Street Southampton SO2 0LD

OCCASIONAL GROUPS

	Description & Location	Characteristics	Openings for Outreach	Contact Person
O1	A neighbourhood group of 10, employed in the professions or business management in Winchester. Both sexes and various ages.	Social classes I, II & III. Lack of interest in the Gospel due to ignorance and confusion, but there is a desire to discuss and clarify religious issues.	Apparently no committed Christians. The Church of England has contact.	Rev W Kingston 20 West Hill Park Winchester SO22 5DY
O2	50 elderly people, mainly widows and widowers, living in flats or bedsitters on the fringes of Southampton. They belong to an Old People's Fellowship. All are retired.	Mixed social classes. Most are lapsed church members. They are more interested in their social life than in spiritual issues.	About 50% would describe themselves as Christians. All the Protestant denominations have contact, and there is a regular Sunday service.	n/a

Total population: 639,000

Estimated number
attending church: 54,000

**Total number not regularly
attending church: 585,000**

Non-attenders as
percentage of population: 92%

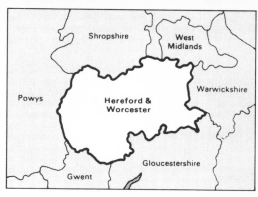

Number of people not regularly attending church:

Age		Sex	
Under 15:	128,000	**Men:**	287,000
15-19:	47,000	**Women:**	298,000
20-29:	82,000		
30-44:	117,000		
45-64:	129,000		
65 or over:	82,000		

SOCIAL/COMMUNITY GROUPS

	Description & Location	Characteristics	Openings for Outreach	Contact Person
S1	200 council house tenants in village near Hereford. Varied ages men and women. Main employment is in factories.	Semi-skilled workers with a working class culture. They are bored and apathetic towards the Church.	5% Christian. The Methodists are in contact.	Mr E Locke Val d'Or Ewyas Harold Hereford HR2 0JB
S2	A council estate at Madley with about 200 inhabitants of all ages, and both sexes. Employed in building trade.	Social group IV. They use the church only for official functions. Children are not encouraged to attend Sunday School. There is no interest in the Gospel.	5% Christian. The Anglican Church is in contact and occasional visits are made by various sects.	Rev W L Paterson Madley Vicarage Hereford HR2 9LP
S3	1,000 people, mainly farmers and their families living in south west Herefordshire. The group includes quite a lot of old people. Men and women.	Social group III. They are most conscious of economic security. Apathy, combined with difficulties of lack of time in the farming industry are blocks to the Gospel.	60% Christian but only nominally. Every house in 13 parishes is being visited by the Anglican Church.	Rev M Edge The Rectory Ewyas Harold Hereford HR2 0EY

HERTFORDSHIRE

Total population: 968,000

Estimated number
attending church: 73,000

**Total number not regularly
attending church:** **895,000**

Non-attenders as
percentage of population: 92%

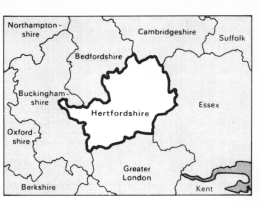

Number of people not regularly attending church:

Age		Sex	
Under 15:	197,000	**Men:**	439,000
15-19:	72,000	**Women:**	456,000
20-29:	125,000		
30-44:	179,000		
45-64:	215,000		
65 or over:	107,000		

SOCIAL/COMMUNITY GROUPS

	Description & Location	Characteristics	Openings for Outreach	Contact Person
S1	Between 2,000 and 3,000 people living in the upper and outer areas of the commuter town of Berkhamsted. Employed as executives in business, government, professional consultancies etc. All ages. Men and women.	Social groups I & II. All well-to-do people, pre-occupied with socio-economic security and the preservation of status quo.	10% Christian. A few are invited to local house groups. There are several Anglican churches in the area and many of other denominations.	Dr John Boyes 13 The Meads Northchurch Berkhamsted Herts HP4 3OX
S2	Many of the 4,300 population of Bovingdon. There is a wide range of employment, but many work with computers. Various ages and both sexes.	Social groups II & III. Most of them see Christianity as irrelevant, and are not conscious of any spiritual needs.	4% are Christian. The Anglican and Baptist churches have contact.	n/a
S3	300 in a 'nice' village in Hertfordshire 20 miles north of London. Most of the population work in London offices. Both sexes and various ages.	Management social group. People are mostly concerned with materialism and their children. Their background, outlook and lack of time are blocks to the Gospel.	5% Christian. Anglican, URC, Methodist and Roman Catholic churches all have contact.	Mr M Cooper 106 Pondcroft Road Knebworth Herts SG3 6DE
S4	About 2,000 people on an estate at Stevenage with mostly young couples and many children. A high percentage of them work with British Aerospace.	Social groups II & III. All are concerned with housing and the lack of facilities on the estate. The young people hardly know what the Church is about.	Less than 1% Christian. A monthly evening service is held in some flats for the elderly. Anglican and Methodist churches have contact.	n/a

SOCIAL/COMMUNITY GROUPS *(continued)* **HERTFORDSHIRE**

Description & Location	Characteristics	Openings for Outreach	Contact Person
S5 The population of villages near Ware. About 500 in each village. Men and women, all ages but many older people. Mainly commuters in manufacturing and service industries.	Management social group II. They are materialistic and the older people are much concerned with their health.	50% nominal Christian, but very few committed. Church of England have contact, and there is work going on among the elderly.	Rev Stephen Motyer The Vicarage Albany, Ware Herts SG11 2HU
S6 A group from about 2,000 households on council estates in Hitchin. The full age range is covered, and there are many old and young people. There is high unemployment.	Social groups IV & V. Their needs are in the areas of social problems, marriage breakdowns, illness and wayward children. There are communication difficulties with the churches. Christians do not speak the same language!	Up to 5% Christian. Those in contact include Strict Baptists, a local Christian house fellowship and the Church of God.	n/a
S7 An estate at New Barnet with mostly council houses and a population of several hundreds of all ages. Men and women.	Social groups III, IV & V. Concerned with employment and their own community. They see Christianity as something for those who are happy with it.	There are Baptist and Anglican churches. Visitation has produced virtually no response.	n/a
S8 The majority of the residents of Carpenders Park, numbering between 5,000 and 6,000. A self contained community of private dwellings. Both sexes, and an above average number of old people. Varied employment.	Social groups are skilled manual and non-manual. There appears to be an unusually high interest in spiritual reality. Ignorance of the Gospel main block to it.	There is no church on the estate but there are some Christians who worship off the estate, about 80 regular church goers. An interdenominational outreach has been started. House groups have been quite successful, and recently 100 attended a community family service in the local school.	Mr Peter Hicks 122 Harrow Way Carpenders Park Watford Herts WD1 5ES
S9 5,000 commuters living around Radlett. Middle class professionals, with executive jobs. All ages. Men and women.	Social group I, mainly commuters. Unwilling to be involved in church life. They are very affluent and lack leisure time.	10% Christian. The Anglican, URC, Methodist and Roman Catholic churches are in contact.	n/a
S10 About 90% of the population around Hoddesdon and Broxbourne. Most of them are families from London or the West Midlands. Mix of age, both sexes. Employed in industry and commerce.	Social group V. They are materialistic and ignorant about Christianity. The church appears to have failed to identify with them in any caring way.	Most church goers are elderly. The churches in Hoddesdon are evangelical and all attempt outreach.	Rev D Read The Manse Middlefield Road Hoddesdon Herts EN11 9ED

Description & Location	Characteristics	Openings for Outreach	Contact Person
S11 1,200 from a former London 'overflow estate' now living on a large housing estate at Tring. All ages, particularly young and old. Most are employed in the building trade or as drivers. Men and women.	Unskilled social group. They are only aware of social needs and are not conscious of spiritual needs. Self-sufficient attitude is a block to the Good News.	1% are Christian. Independent Evangelical Fellowship are working with them in regular and varied activities, and Roman Catholic church is in contact.	Rev I Walker 25 Shugars Green Tring Herts HP23 5EH
S12 A housing estate at West Watford with a population of 3,000. In a variety of employment. Mainly families with all age groups represented.	Social groups III, IV & V. Their main concerns are unemployment and their relative poverty. Many have never been to church and have only a vague and false idea of it from the media.	1% Christian. There is a non-denominational fellowship. Baptist and Roman Catholic churches in contact.	Pastor Frank Wren 62 Harford Drive Watford Herts WD1 3DG

ETHNIC/LINGUISTIC GROUPS

Description & Location	Characteristics	Openings for Outreach	Contact Person
E1 A group of 200-300 Asians living in St Albans. They work as engineers, shopkeepers and in local offices etc. Most have large families.	They come from India and Pakistan. 40% can read English. Their mother tongues are Hindi, Urdu and Bengali and their religion is Hinduism or Islam. The Moslems have their own school and maintain their own customs, and many of the women have poor spoken English.	Only one family are Christian. There is a CMS Missionary who helps.	n/a
E2 4,000 mostly Pakistani living in poorer areas in Watford. They work in factories, shops and sub post offices. They are mainly in families, with all age groups represented.	All the children at school read English and 50% of the adults. Their native language is Urdu and their religion is Islam.	1% are Christian. A group of pastors are trying to obtain a missionary for them.	n/a
E3 1,000 people in a prosperous Jewish community in the suburb of Hadley Wood. Employed in the professions and in business. All ages. Men and women.	Their mother tongue is English. There is antipathy to the Church.	Less than 1% are Christian. Churches include them in general parochial ministry.	n/a

OCCASIONAL GROUPS

Description & Location	Characteristics	Openings for Outreach	Contact Person
O1 30 to 50 members of a model engineering club and 100 members of football clubs at Hitchin. Their work is varied. They are all men, and the footballers in particular are in younger age group.	Social groups III, IV & V. They fill their time with their hobbies. Their clubs meet on Sundays.	The number of Christians is not known. There is a local Anglican parish church.	n/a

Total population: 856,000

Estimated number
attending church: 45,000

**Total number not regularly
attending church: 811,000**

Non-attenders as
percentage of population: 95%

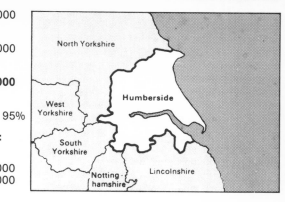

Number of people not regularly attending church:

Age		Sex	
Under 15:	187,000	**Men:**	397,000
15-19:	65,000	**Women:**	414,000
20-29:	113,000		
30-44:	146,000		
45-64:	187,000		
65 or over:	113,000		

SOCIAL/COMMUNITY GROUPS

	Description & Location	Characteristics	Openings for Outreach	Contact Person
S1	2,500 poorer council house tenants on an estate at Driffield. Most are employed in agriculture, small factories or shops. Men and women and large numbers of both old and young people.	Unskilled, they are kept together by social identity. They suffer from poor housing and much family distress. Their image of the Church is of a middle class institution.	5% are Christian. The Church of England have contact and there is individual witness by the few Christians among them.	Rev M Simons The Vicarage Driffield Yorks YO25 7DU
S2	A large group in Hull living in older property in the city centre. Predominantly young, in responsible jobs in the service and production industries. Both sexes.	Social groups II & III. They are concerned mostly with status, their professions and family improvement. They see the Church as irrelevant.	Less than 5% Christian. There are a variety of churches but only fringe contact.	Rev M Vernon St Johns Vicarage Clough Road Kingston-upon-Hull HW6 7RA
S3	The population of the rural areas of Humberside. Large numbers of older people who have worked on the land. Besides agriculture they are employed at the power station and as drivers.	Social groups II, III & IV. They are concerned generally with agriculture and survival. There is a great deal of superstition and misunderstanding about the Church.	1% Christian. The Church of England and the Methodists have contact.	Rev P S Lindeck The Vicarage Reedness Goole Humberside DN14 8MG
S4	The large traditional working class population of the city of Hull, living in terraced houses of the inner city and in vast council estates. Employed as labourers, in factories, the railways, building, the docks or unemployed. Normal age distribution.	Social groups III, IV & V. Secular working class attitudes and 'folk faith' are barriers to the Gospel.	Only 5% of the population of 250,000 are Christian. All denominations have been in the city for 150 years but the impact has declined since the 20s.	Rev D G Attfield 388 Southcoates Lane Hull HU9 3UN

ISLE OF WIGHT

Total population:	119,000
Estimated number attending church:	12,000
Total number not regularly attending church:	**107,000**
Non-attenders as percentage of population:	90%

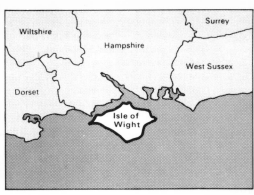

Number of people not regularly attending church:

Age		Sex	
Under 15:	20,000	**Men:**	50,000
15-19:	7,000	**Women:**	57,000
20-29:	13,000		
30-44:	17,000		
45-64:	27,000		
65 or over:	23,000		

Total population: 1,486,000

Estimated number
attending church: 110,000

**Total number not regularly
attending church: 1,376,000**

Non-attenders as
percentage of population: 93%

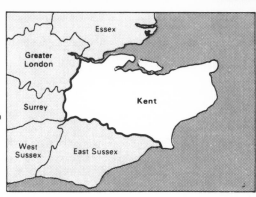

Number of people not regularly attending church:

Age		Sex	
Under 15:	316,000	**Men:**	674,000
15-19:	110,000	**Women:**	702,000
20-29:	193,000		
30-44:	248,000		
45-64:	303,000		
65 or over:	206,000		

SOCIAL/COMMUNITY GROUPS

	Description & Location	Characteristics	Openings for Outreach	Contact Person
S1	3,000 people on a recently built housing estate at Folkestone. They are young to middle aged, employed for the most part with work concerning cross channel traffic and other clerical work. Men and women.	Non-manual, social group III. All are of similar age and income bracket, buying their own homes. They are career conscious and very concerned with money and possessions. They think the Church is irrelevant.	5% Christian. There is a Church of England and general outreach by Sunday School teachers and members.	Rev P Webber St Johns Vicarage 4 Cornwallis Ave Folkestone Kent CT19 5JA
S2	4,000 living in a large housing estate in Barden. Employed as factory workers or cleaners. Large numbers of old and young people.	Skilled and unskilled manual workers. There is a general feeling that living a good life is enough, and no sense of non-material needs.	2% Christian. Outreach by 'Tell Tonbridge 84' mission. The Church of England, URC and Pentecostal churches are in contact.	Rev D B Kitley 35 Waterloo Road Tonbridge Kent TN9 2SW
S3	Two post-war council estates 2-3 miles from Chatham, housing about 12,000, mostly manual workers in the dockyard or oil refinery. There is a full age range. Men and women.	Social groups III, IV & V. Concerned with unemployment and poor medical facilities in area. They consider that the Church is middle class and intellectual. The Church is used for baptisms, weddings and funerals.	Less than 1% Christian. Church of England have some contact. Regular Sunday services are held in the local school and a full time community worker is employed.	Mr Ken Gardiner 289 Walderslade Road Chatham Kent ME5 0NU
S4	200 people on a new housing estate at Broadstairs. Houses all owner-occupied by teachers, the self-employed, shop and office workers. Many young married people with children.	Non-manual and skilled manual social group III. Life is comfortable and their general outlook is materialistic.	5% Christian. The Church of England and Roman Catholic church have contact, but no special outreach is being undertaken.	Ms Joan Burrows 14 Upton Road Broadstairs Kent CT10 2AS

	Description & Location	Characteristics	Openings for Outreach	Contact Person
S5	About 3,000 living on new housing estates in Hythe. Employed in offices and as teachers, nurses, builders and power station staff. Large numbers of old and young people.	Social groups I, II & III. They are materialistic, and spiritually self-satisfied.	10% attend church but perhaps 2% Christian. One church building shared by Anglicans and Roman Catholics.	Mr M E Baker 47 Palmarsh Ave Hythe Kent CT21 6NR
S6	A group of upper middle class, mainly middle aged people living in Sevenoaks. By profession they are directors, bankers, stock brokers etc.	Social groups I & II. They have all that they want materially, and are not aware of any other needs.	Number of Christians not known. Anglicans probably have most contact.	Rev J Tattersall The Manse 1 Hillside Road Sevenoaks Kent TN13 3XJ
S7	4,000 people living in the residential area of Chalk. Mixed age range, some commute to London and others work in local industry.	Social group IV. The majority just drift through life and are apathetic about the Gospel and religion.	Up to 6% are Christian. There is a local Anglican parish church undertaking outreach.	n/a
S8	10,000 living in the locality of Wilmington. Full age range and a variety of employment.	Social groups I, II & III. They are concerned with money, employment, peace, health and security. They have no real concept of God, and their outlook is materialistic.	4% Christian. There is door-to-door visitation by the Anglican church and FIEC.	Mr Edward C Doe 48 Leyton Cross Road Wilmington Kent DA2 7AW
S9	A large council estate at Orpington with 5,000 mainly young or middle aged people. A small percentage commute to London, but most work locally in variety of jobs.	Social groups III, IV & V. They have little or no sense of the Christian faith. Many would regard the Church as having little relevance.	3% or less Christian. The Council of Churches has founded a Church of Unity. There is no other organized witness.	n/a
S10	The inhabitants of 2,000 homes on a private estate at Falconwood. Employed in sales, gas engineering or clerical. There are no elderly people, but a large number of children.	Social groups III, non-manual and skilled manual. Their concern is in getting better material standards. Most are ignorant of the Gospel and consider it irrelevant to their lives.	10% are Christian. The Anglicans have discussion groups and there is house visitation and other activities.	Mr K J Newell 100 Cumberland Avenue Welling Kent DA16 2PU
S11	4,000 people on mainly council estate at Dartford, working in factories or commuting to London. Mixed ages. Men and women.	Social groups III, IV & V. They are concerned about work, money, holidays and bingo. They are apathetic about spiritual things.	3% Christian. The Church of England, Pentecostal and non-conformist churches have the most contact.	n/a

Description & Location	Characteristics	Openings for Outreach	Contact Person
S12 220 people living on a council housing estate at Hawkhurst. All families with children. Employment is very varied.	Social groups IV & V. Their needs are purely material. They are kept away from the Gospel by materialism, entertainment, the media and their image of the Church.	2% Christians. The Baptist and the Anglican are in contact, and there has been visitation.	Rev John G Hart The Manse Western Road Hawkhurst Kent TN18 4BT

ETHNIC/LINGUISTIC GROUPS

Description & Location	Characteristics	Openings for Outreach	Contact Person
E1 Several thousand Sikh Indians, some from East Africa but the majority from their native Punjab, who have settled at Chatham. Large numbers of old and young people. The men work in factories and the women in the fields or sweat shops.	50% can read English. Their mother tongue is Punjabi, and their religion Sikh. Their main concern is to master the English language. They are unwilling to enter a church, and church people are reluctant to go to Indian houses.	No Christians in group, and no churches in contact.	n/a
E2 There are 6,000 to 7,000 immigrants in Gravesend. They came originally from Pakistan and India. The children were born in this country. They work in factories or small businesses. Mixed age range.	60% can read English. Their mother tongue is mostly Punjabi and their religion is Sikh. Blocks to the Gospel are mainly cultural.	Less than 1% Christian. There is at present no outreach.	n/a
E3 Several thousand immigrants living in Dartford. Many from Pakistan, Mauritius and Malaya, with some Singhalese. Some Africans from Uganda and Kenya. Many work in hospitals as nurses, doctors, porters and cleaners. Others are shopkeepers. Many old and young people.	90% speak English. There are various mother tongues and the religions include Sikh, Hinduism, Islam and Buddhism. Christianity is an alien religion to most of them.	Perhaps 1-2% Christians. Those from Mauritius are nominal Roman Catholics and some from Africa are nominal Protestants. There are local churches and a Chaplain and Christian Union at the hospitals.	Mr Edward C Doe 48 Leyton Cross Road Wilmington Kent DA2 7AW

OCCASIONAL GROUPS

Description & Location	Characteristics	Openings for Outreach	Contact Person
O1 A sports club at Welling with 300 members, mainly families and young people. Employed as teachers, self employed or clerical. Men and women.	Social group III, skilled manual and non-manual. They are concerned with pleasure and social enjoyment. They do not consider religion relevant to their lives.	Number of Christians is not known. There is an Evangelical church nearby.	Mr K J Newell 100 Cumberland Avenue Welling Kent DA16 2PU

Description & Location	Characteristics	Openings for Outreach	Contact Person
O2 50 people in the village of Hawkhurst who meet several evenings a week for friendship and drinks in the local public house. There are older teenagers to young adults in various forms of employment. Men and women.	Social groups IV & V. Their main concerns are material advancement and unemployment. Materialism, ignorance and peer pressure keep them from the Gospel.	There are no Christians. There is some visitation to the homes.	Rev John G Hart The Manse Western Road Hawkhurst Kent TN18 4BT
O3 A Women's Institute at Penshurst with 40 members, mostly over 60 and all retired. All female.	Social group III. Occupied with their social lives and entertainment, they have no habit of church attendance.	2% Christian. No known outreach. There is an Anglican church in contact.	n/a
O4 Shifting population of Army families at Hythe. About 300 men, women and children in the younger age group. Husbands in Army; wives work in shops, offices etc.	Covers all social groups. Most of them are materially well off. They are too wealthy and too well looked after by the army to bother with the Gospel.	Some nominal Christians. There is a church building shared by Anglicans and Roman Catholics. There is a great need for evangelism and youth work.	Mr M E Baker 7 Palmarsh Avenue Hythe Kent CT21 6NR
O5 A group of about 15 foreign students in Broadstairs. All are young men and women 18-30 years.	All students learning English. Many are French Roman Catholics.	5% Christian. The Baptists are in contact. Mission work needed, perhaps in Bible study groups.	Rev M C Jones 13 Brassey Ave Broadstairs Kent
O6 30 senior citizens, mostly widows, living at St Peters, Broadstairs. Some are in sheltered accommodation. Mainly women. Retired from Civil Service, local government etc.	Social group III. They are concerned about loneliness, frailty and inability to manage their property and gardens. They have managed so far without the Gospel, and are reluctant to admit to their fears and need.	4% Christians. The Baptist church and Pentecostal church have various activities for them.	Ms Joan Burrows 4 Upton Road Broadstairs Kent CT10 2AS
O7 The residents of the many nursing homes at Whitstable. There are between 8 and 60 in each home. Both sexes but all old and retired.	Social group III non-manual. They are very conscious of loneliness and fear of death. There is a great need for friendship. Their faith derives from their experiences at Sunday School.	10 Christian. All denominations have contact.	Rev C N Speed 108 Clare Road Whitstable Kent CT5 2EP
O8 40 members of a Mothers and Toddlers group at Wilmington. Also 50-60 mothers of younger schoolchildren who meet collecting their children from school. All young women.	Social groups I, II & III. They are concerned about material well being, security and health. There is general apathy and lack of conviction of sin.	Less than 3% of the school mothers are Christian. Up to 25% Mothers and Toddlers group are Christian. The group is run by a local Church. The mothers of the schoolchildren attend special services at the school at Christmas and Harvest. Anglicans and FIEC have most contact.	Mr Edward C Doe 48 Leyton Cross Road Wilmington Kent DA2 7AW

Description & Location	Characteristics	Openings for Outreach	Contact Person
O9 Workers at the local hospital at Wilmington, numbering about 1,000, mainly younger people of both sexes.	Social groups I, II & III. They are materialistic, and apathy keeps them from the Gospel	2-3% Christian. Evangelistic chaplain and team serve the hospital. Anglicans and FIEC in contact.	Mr Edward C Doe 48 Leyton Cross Road Wilmington Kent DA2 7AW
O10 30 men and women in a group of over 60s, all retired, meeting monthly for friendship and conversation in the village of Penshurst.	Social group IV. Their needs are mainly social. The language of the Bible and liturgic worship are a block to knowing Jesus Christ.	2% Christian. There is an Anglican church in area.	n/a
O11 30-50 members of a village football club. Varied age range and some women included.	Semi-skilled and unskilled workers, bound by their interest in sport. Their aspirations are materialistic and they are ignorant of spiritual values.	No Christians in group, and apparently none in contact with them.	Mr John G Hart The Manse Western Road Hawkhurst Kent TN18 4BT
O12 About 24 playgroup workers and their husbands, who work mainly in management.	Social group II. They are occupied with community service and have no sense of spiritual need.	12% Christian. Church of England in contact.	Mr J Brandham 57 Hever Wood Road West Kingsdown Sevenoaks Kent TN15 6HW
O13 A group of 20 teenagers at Leigh. At school, local colleges or serving apprenticeships etc. Both sexes.	Social groups IV & V. They desire to be free from adult direction. They are kept from the Gospel by peer group pressure, and difficulty of worship in an 'alien' culture.	10% Christian. There is a Church of England, but no youth work undertaken.	Rev G C M Miles The Vicarage Leigh Tonbridge Kent TN11 8QJ

LANCASHIRE

Total population:	1,384,000
Estimated number attending church:	157,000
Total number not regularly attending church:	**1,227,000**
Non-attenders as percentage of population:	89%

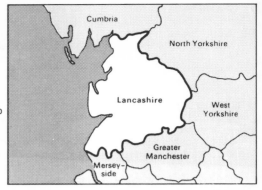

Number of people not regularly attending church:

Age		Sex	
Under 15:	270,000	**Men:**	589,000
15-19:	98,000	**Women:**	638,000
20-29:	160,000		
30-44:	221,000		
45-64:	282,000		
65 or over:	196,000		

SOCIAL/COMMUNITY GROUPS

	Description & Location	Characteristics	Openings for Outreach	Contact Person
S1	A group of 60-70 young men and women all employed in farming in a rural area at the village of Bilsborrow.	Concerned with social life and with the humanitarian needs of the world. Too busy with Young Farmer Club to bother with Church.	2% are committed Christians. Free Methodist Church in contact.	n/a
S2	Young married couples with one or two children living in restored property near the outskirts of the village of Trawden. There are about 60 or 70, employed in engineering, teaching, shops and nursing.	Non manual and skilled manual workers, preoccupied with cars, comfortable homes and money.	Number of Christians not known. Church of England and Independent Methodists have made contact.	Rev P Allson The Vicarage Burnley Road Trawden Lancs BB8 8PN
S3	A group of 20 women all under 30, one parent families with small children living on a small council housing estate at Rossendale. They work part-time, or as home workers.	Unskilled, but some of them have not reached their educational potential. All have financial and emotional problems. There is apathy towards the Church.	None are Christians, but the Vicar and church members are in contact.	Rev G R Loxham St Anne's Vicarage Ashworth Road Edgeside Waterfoot Rossendale Lancs BB4 9JE
S4	1,600 young married couples and their children who have settled on an estate at Tottington. They have come from other areas and are first time buyers. Most are engaged in office work.	Non manual workers, social group III. They are concerned about their financial needs and friendship. Their outlook is materialistic.	5% Christian. The Methodist church is in contact. There is also a Church of England.	Rev Alan Reeve 1 Booth Way Tottington Bury Lancs BL8 3JL

Description & Location	Characteristics	Openings for Outreach	Contact Person
S5 3,000 unemployed men living in a 'matriarchal society' on a corporation housing estate in Bootle. They spend their time digging the allotment or decorating. Mixed ages.	They have no purpose in life and consider the Church irrelevant to them.	Less than 1% Christian. The Baptist Church is in contact. There is also a Roman Catholic church in the area.	Rev R Spurin 157 St Oswalds Lane Netherton Bootle Lancs L30 5QF
S6 2,500 people living on two estates in Burnley. There is a complete age range and most of them are employed on production work. Men and women.	Social groups IV & V. There is a lack of social cohesion and concern. They cannot understand the value of the Gospel.	1% Christian. There are churches in the area, but none attempting outreach.	Rev J G Brockbank Haberghan Vicarage Burnley Lancs BB12 6LH
S7 Occupants of a high rise council estate at Rochdale, numbering 2,000 people of all ages. Engaged in factory work. Men and women.	Social group IV. They are conscious of the need for work and money. Their culture and previous bad experiences keep them from the Church.	1% Christian. The Methodists are in contact and there is a community worker.	n/a
S8 1,200 council house tenants at Darwen. Mainly young families employed in unskilled work in the paper industry.	Social group V. Their culture is working class, and they do not see the relevance of the Church to people like them.	1% Christian. There is pastoral contact from the Church of England.	n/a
S9 A growing group of people near Lancaster who have made enough money to retire to the country or commute. They are mainly older professional people.	Social class I. Very self-sufficient group, with no material needs, and not conscious of spiritual ones.	Very few Christians. There are several local churches and the Anglican and Methodist churches are most involved in outreach.	n/a
S10 A group of 1,500 mainly young people living on a fairly new housing estate at Helmshore. Men and women in a variety of employment.	Social groups I, II & III. Indifferent to the Gospel.	2% Christian. Churches include Roman Catholic, Church of England, Methodist. Outreach by the clergy and lay workers.	Rev S L McQuoid 7 Gorse Grove Helmshore Rossendale Lancs BB4 4JE
S11 1,100-1,500 people living in small private developments on the edge of Rossendale. Many children and teenagers. Employed in management, commerce and blue collar industrial work.	Social groups II & III. Their main need is for local friendship and support. Their lifestyles affirm their materialistic values.	No known Christians or outreach.	Rev A Brazier 38 Turnpike Newchurch Rossendale Lancs BB4 9DU

Description & Location	Characteristics	Openings for Outreach	Contact Person
S12 1,000 to 1,500 in older or council housing. Most of them are employed in production work and all are on lower incomes.	Social groups IV and V. There is a lack of local cohesion and concern and it is difficult to convince them about the Gospel.	The number of Christians is not known.	Rev J Brockbank Habergham Vicarage Burnley BB12 6LH
S13 The entire population of Middleton. 53,000 people, mainly manual workers but there is quite high unemployment, especially among young people.	Social groups III & V. Many of the people have the wrong ideas about the Church. There is a lack of spiritual power and authority in many local churches.	Less than 1% Christian. The Baptist and an independent fellowship are in contact and outreach is being undertaken by a small group.	Mr Paul Morley 7 Wordsworth Road Boarshaw Middleton Manchester Lancs M24 2PD
S14 The residents of several housing estates in Blackpool. Some 2,000-5,000 in each. Mainly young families.	Social groups I, II & III. Their needs are primarily material.	2% Christian. No known outreach.	n/a
S15 450 families living on two estates at Blackburn. A large number are young and are employed as representatives and in sales and advisory work.	Social groups II & III. Many are on short term contracts and do not stay very long.	10% Christian. The Church of England and the Methodists are in contact. House groups and visiting are needed.	Mr Roy Braithwaite St James Vicarage Cromer Place Blackburn Lancs BB1 8EL

ETHNIC/LINGUISTIC GROUPS

Description & Location	Characteristics	Openings for Outreach	Contact Person
E1 20,000 Asian immigrants to Blackburn from India and Bangladesh. Many young people, largely unemployed but some work in shops or small businesses.	30% can read English. Their mother tongues are Gujerati and Urdu, and their religion Islam. Their greatest need is for housing and employment. A firm adherence to Islam keeps them from the Gospel.	No known outreach and no Christians in the group.	Mr M J Cleaves 20 Gorse Road Blackburn Lancs BB2 6LZ
E2 A group of about 600 Pakistanis living in a small area of terraced houses at Preston. Their employment is mainly manual, and there is a mix of ages.	60% can read English and their mother tongue is Urdu. Their religion is Islam. Their main need is for employment, otherwise they are firmly self-sufficient. A house in the area serves as a mosque.	No known Christians. Local churches hope to reach some with Mission England.	Rev T A Roberts Fishergate Baptist Church Charnley Street Preston Lancs PR1 2UR

OCCASIONAL GROUPS

Description & Location	Characteristics	Openings for Outreach	Contact Person
O1 58 members of an Air Training Corps at Blackburn. Adult leaders and 50 young men and women between the ages of 14 and 20. They meet twice weekly. The adults are mainly in management jobs.	Social groups II & III. They are most anxious about their future security. They see the Church as old fashioned 'do gooders'.	5% Christian. An Anglican chaplain has been newly appointed.	Rev Wotherspoon Witton Vicarage Buncer Lane Blackburn Lancs BB2 0SY

	Description & Location	Characteristics	Openings for Outreach	Contact Person
O2	At Preston there are 300 nurses in training, living in residential homes or scattered in flats etc. Most of them are young women.	Social group III. They are conscious of the strain of coping with suffering and death. The main blocks to experiencing the Gospel is the secularisation of the world of medicine and unresolved ethical dilemmas.	30% Christian, but few committed. Roman Catholic and Anglican churches have contact. There is outreach from some of the nurses and part-time chaplains.	Rev J Burns Christ Church Vicarage 6 Watling Street Rd Fulwood Preston Lancs PR2 4DY
O3	A total of between 300 and 500 young people in teenage street groups in Rossendale. The majority are boys but there are some girls.	Social groups IV & V. They need a base and activity for themselves, and acceptance by adults. Their age, rebellious attitudes and culture keep them from the Good News.	No known Christians. There are churches in the area, but no-one attempting outreach. Street contact or club with 'drop-in' facilities needed.	Rev A Brazier 38 Turnpike Newchurch Rossendale Lancs BB4 9DU
O4	A group of 25 young parents at Skelmersdale, keen on starting a children's playgroup. They are mainly housewives and unemployed men.	Social groups IV & V. Concerned with the needs of their children. They have a fear of being 'got at' by the Church.	4% Christian. There is outreach from a local minister. They need help and support from Christians.	Rev H D Evans The Manse 34 Whitburn Skelmersdale Heaton Bolton Lancs WN8 8HQ
O5	Workers in the town centre of Bolton. Between 2,000 and 3,000 shopkeepers, typists, salesmen, journalists etc., mostly young.	Social group III non-manual. They are too preoccupied with work and their busy lives to respond to the Gospel.	2% Christian. Churches of all denominations are in the area. There is need for outreach and activities at lunch times.	Mr Kevin Wilson 49 Lonsdale Road Heaton Bolton Lancs BL1 4PW

LEICESTERSHIRE

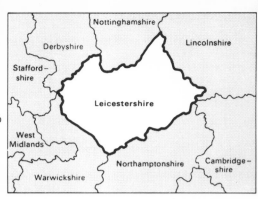

Total population:	861,000
Estimated number attending church:	65,000
Total number not regularly attending church:	**796,000**
Non-attenders as percentage of population:	92%

Number of people not regularly attending church:

Age		Sex	
Under 15:	175,000	**Men:**	390,000
15-19:	64,000	**Women:**	406,000
20-29:	127,000		
30-44:	151,000		
45-64:	175,000		
65 or over:	104,000		

SOCIAL/COMMUNITY GROUPS

	Description & Location	Characteristics	Openings for Outreach	Contact Person
S1	4,000 people in upper working and middle class families in the growing village of Rothley. Many are young and most are employed in banking, engineering, insurance, or textiles.	Social groups I, II & III. Materialistic and not aware of the need for salvation. Their past church involvements would have had negative effect.	8% Christian. The Anglicans and Baptists have mother and toddlers groups, lunches, and coffee and dinner evenings. There is also visitation and ventures connected with Mission England.	Rev Stuart Clarke 17 Rockhill Drive Mount Sorrel Leicestershire LE12 7DS
S2	Several hundred people who live in four small country villages in Rutland. They are employed in the professions and businesses in nearby towns, and in local farming. Mostly middle-aged people of both sexes.	Social groups I & II. They are kept from the Gospel by apathy, affluence and agnosticism.	5% Christian. The rector of the local Anglican church and a Methodist lay worker are undertaking outreach.	Canon A M S Wilson Preston Rectory Oakham Rutland Leicestershire LE15 9NN
S3	About 2,000 people in families in new development areas at Shepshed. Employed in management and industry, and in technical and computing work.	Social group II. They have settled in the country to isolate themselves from their work. Self-satisfied and affluent, they tend to disregard Christianity.	2% Christian. Contact is very limited, but some door-to-door visiting by the Church of England.	n/a
S4	2,500 men and women living on council estates at Ashby de la Zouch. Mixed ages, employed in mining, factories or transport.	Social groups IV & V. They feel overawed and threatened by official-dom and the apparently middle class structure of the Church. The Gospel has been presented to them in too cerebral a manner.	Less than 1% Christian. There is general parish outreach and there is also a Congregational church.	Rev L Dutton Trinity Vicarage Station Road Ashby de la Zouch Leicestershire LE6 5GL

	Description & Location	Characteristics	Openings for Outreach	Contact Person
S5	A group of about 30 young men and women at Fleckney. Unemployed or still at school.	Unskilled social group. They appear to have wrong conceptions about the Gospel — they see it as 'sissy' and 'religious'.	No Christians among them. There are occasional Christian concerts, and personal evangelism is attempted. Baptist church has most contact.	Rev W P Kearney 4 Leicester Road Fleckney Leicester LE8 0BF
S6	There are about 6,000 students living in halls of residence around the city. Most are between 18 and 21. Men and women.	Social groups I to III. They are concerned with the material needs of themselves and the world and they have a humanistic philosophy. Little interest in or understanding of Christian truths.	4% Christian. Outreach by UCCF and limited church activity by the Baptist, Anglican and FIEC churches.	Mr Brian Blacklock 79 Romway Road Leicester LE5 5SE
S7	A council housing estate at Leicester with a population of 1,200. A full age range, and employed in hosiery, shoe manufacture and engineering.	Mainly classes III, IV & V. They consider that the churches have a middle class ethos and a narrow image.	5% Christian. Traditional church activities by Roman Catholics, Methodists, Church of England and Salvation Army.	Rev G Hainsworth 8 Bursdon Close Leicester LE3 6PG
S8	About 450 people who have settled in small villages near Lutterworth. Mainly married with adolescent children. Working in light industries or the more lucrative professions.	Social classes I, II & III. Main needs are material and economic survival. They suspect that religion is true and wish it were not. Others have intellectual difficulties, largely false but bolstered by the media.	The number of Christians is difficult to estimate. The church is used for 'rites of passage' or on sentimental occasions.	Rev P Etchells Ashby Magna Vicarage Lutterworth Leicestershire LE17 5NF

OCCASIONAL GROUPS

O1	A group of 40 to 50 elderly people, mainly women, meeting weekly in Shepshed. All retired.	Social group III. Most conscious needs are for security, care and friendship. They are very tied up with the traditions of the past.	20% Christian. The Church of England and the Baptists have personal contact and arrange meetings.	Rev David Hughes 10 Charnwood Rd Shepshed Loughborough Leicestershire LE12 9QF
O2	About 20 younger women in a Young Wives group at Fleckney, meeting monthly. They are housewives or employed in clerical work.	Social group III, non-manual. They accept some sort of 'social gospel', but have not come to terms with sin and salvation.	Number of Christians not known. The group is based on the Anglican church.	Rev W P Kearney 4 Leicester Road Fleckney Leicester LE8 0BF

LINCOLNSHIRE

Total population:	552,000
Estimated number attending church:	62,000
Total number not regularly attending church:	**490,000**
Non-attenders as percentage of population:	89%

Number of people not regularly attending church:

Age		Sex	
Under 15:	103,000	**Men:**	245,000
15-19:	39,000	**Women:**	245,000
20-29:	73,000		
30-44:	93,000		
45-64:	113,000		
65 or over:	69,000		

SOCIAL/COMMUNITY GROUPS

	Description & Location	Characteristics	Openings for Outreach	Contact Person
S1	8,500 people living on a council housing estate on the outskirts of Lincoln. Employed in factories, shops or unemployed. Large numbers of both young and old people.	Semi-skilled and unskilled. They are concerned with their material needs and there is a lack of belief in God.	5% Christian. Community Centre activities only. The churches in the area are Anglican, URC, Methodist and Roman Catholics.	n/a

OCCASIONAL GROUPS

O1	Up to 100 people connected with a pre-school playgroup in Stamford. Some men but mainly young women. Employed in teaching, engineering and local service industries.	Social groups III & IV. They are almost completely separated from the churches but need each other for mutual support etc.	15% Christian. There is contact with the Methodist church through the leaders of the group.	n/a

Total population: 1,511,000

Estimated number
attending church: 183,000

**Total number not regularly
attending church: 1,328,000**

Non-attenders as
percentage of population: 88%

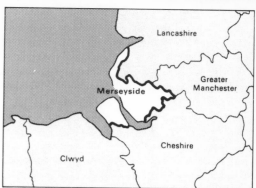

Number of people not regularly attending church:

Age		Sex	
Under 15:	292,000	**Men:**	651,000
15-19:	106,000	**Women:**	677,000
20-29:	199,000		
30-44:	239,000		
45-64:	306,000		
65 or over:	186,000		

SOCIAL/COMMUNITY GROUPS

	Description & Location	Characteristics	Openings for Outreach	Contact Person
S1	About 3,000 men and women living in 'bed-sits' at Birkenhead. Many are old but there are a number in 20s and 30s. Most are pensioners or unemployed.	Social group III. All need friendship and hope for the future. They feel that they are not loved or wanted.	Less than 1% are Christian. Outreach is very ineffective. Church of England in contact.	Rev D S Allister Christ Church Vicarage 7 Palm Grove Birkenhead L43 1TE
S2	4,000 residents of an estate at St Helens. All ages and employed mainly at supervisor level.	Non-manual or skilled manual. They have a distrust of the Church and a general lack of interest in religion.	1% Christian. The churches in the area are Methodist, Church of England and Independent Evangelical Fellowship, though many of the group are of Roman Catholic background. The Evangelical Fellowship visit door-to-door.	Mr A W Bridge 301 Old Road Ashton-in-Makerfield Wigan WN4 9TS
S3	A minimum of 1,500 elderly men and women in 160 homes in Southport. All are retired.	All have the problem of loneliness.	5% Christian. There have been various evangelistic approaches.	Mr T G Ellis 15a Lulworth Road Southport Merseyside PR8 2AS

OCCASIONAL GROUPS

O1	A group of up to 40 unemployed young people in Wallasey. Some women, but mainly men, meeting regularly in small groups.	Social groups IV & V. There is a great need for a purpose in life.	5% Christian. URC and Roman Catholic churches have contact.	Mr E A Funnell 11 Lymington Road Wallasey Merseyside L44 3EG

Description & Location	Characteristics	Openings for Outreach	Contact Person
O2 28 men and women in a local History Group in the Everton area of Liverpool. Mostly elderly. Many disabled and unemployed.	Social groups IV & V. There is need for compassion and support. The churches do not show any interest in them.	A few are Christians. The Anglican church has most contact.	Dr D Ben Rees 32 Garth Drive Liverpool L8 6HW
O3 A left-wing group of German Democratic Republic — Britain (Liverpool Branch). About 45 members, mixed men and women. Many of them are retired.	Social group III. They are very interested in and tolerant of religion, but have a poor opinion of the Church in Britain.	No known Christians. The secretary of the group is a Presbyterian minister. They have had a one day school on Martin Luther.	Dr D Ben Rees 32 Garth Drive Liverpool L8 6HW
O4 Men and women engaged in various social activities in the poorer parts of Liverpool, including The Centre for the Aged, Cultural Community Centre, and The Orange Lodge. Mainly middle-aged and elderly. High proportion of unemployed.	Social group III. There is concern about employment and care for the large population of elderly in the area. Church seems irrelevant and unable to help with their social problems.	5% Christian. The Anglican Church has most contact.	Rev Dr G A Catherall 55 Belgrave Road Liverpool L17 7AQ

Total population:	705,000
Estimated number attending church:	52,000
Total number not regularly attending church:	**653,000**
Non-attenders as percentage of population:	93%

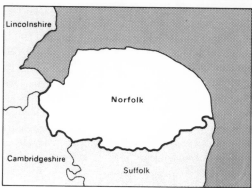

Number of people not regularly attending church:

Age		Sex	
Under 15:	137,000	**Men:**	320,000
15-19:	52,000	**Women:**	333,000
20-29:	91,000		
30-44:	118,000		
45-64:	150,000		
65 or over:	105,000		

SOCIAL/COMMUNITY GROUPS

	Description & Location	Characteristics	Openings for Outreach	Contact Person
S1	About 200 men and women living in council houses in villages around Yarmouth. Full age range.	Semi-skilled. Only concerned with the basic needs of life. They see the Church as archaic, middle class and unattractive.	Very few Christians. Anglican church has most contact.	n/a
S2	300 gypsies and travellers on a permanent site at Norwich. There are a large number of children and teenagers. The parents are engaged in scrap metal or hawking.	Social group V. All feel misunderstood and unaccepted by society.	No known Christians although some have Roman Catholic background. No one is trying to reach them.	Mr Les Stebbings Associate Evangelist Pocket Testament League 3 Lubbock Close Norwich NR2 3QY
S3	Council house tenants in low price housing near Swaffham. 350 men and women of all ages in manual work, but a number are unemployed.	Social group V. Most conscious of material needs, and need pastoral help in marriage break-ups etc. A general dullness about spiritual things. Church services outside their culture.	1% Christian. All totally covered by visiting local Anglican church, and well represented in Sunday School.	Canon D G W Green South Pickenham Rectory Swaffham Norfolk PE37 8DS
S4	About 2,750 retired professional or business people in certain estates and 'good' roads at Sheringham. Some do unpaid charity work.	Social group I. They enjoy the 'good life' of retirement after years of not needing God.	About 10% Christian. The Baptists are engaged in outreach and counselling etc. Anglican and Methodist churches also in contact.	Pastor Derrick Tickner The Manse 7 Cremer's Drift Sheringham Norfolk NR26 8HX
S5	300 men and women from three villages near Fakenham. 60% are retired. Wide range of employment.	Social groups I, II & III. All good, believing, practising Christians but generally not attending church. They know God loves them and helps them.	All nominally Christian. Good Christian neighbours. Local parish churches are covered, by rector. Nearby Methodist and Roman Catholic churches also have contact.	n/a

	Description & Location	Characteristics	Openings for Outreach	Contact Person
S6	Young marrieds forming a quarter of the population around Thetford. They have various occupations and tend to live on new council estates.	Non-manual class III. Each household is insulated from its neighbours since there is little communication between them.	Under 1% Christian. There is no known Christian outreach. Anglicans have most contact.	Rev J Andrews Mundford Rectory Thetford Norfolk IP26 5DS
S7	Five villages in rural South Norfolk, each with a population of between 250 and 600. Many are retired and there are very few young people. Variety of employment.	All social groups are represented in the villages. About 15% have some church connection. There is apathy and a deliberate rejection of the Christian facts of faith.	3% Christians. There is outreach mainly from the Church of England with aid from other Christians, especially the Baptists.	Rev J Lister Winfarthing Rectory Diss Norfolk IP22 2EA
S8	500 on a large council estate at Kings Lynn which includes a large number of old people. Most work in factories, especially canning.	Social group V. Material needs are their main concern. The Church is irrelevant to them.	Less than 1% Christian. Open Brethren are undertaking outreach with Sunday School and work with old folks.	Mr Archie Hall 69 King George V Avenue Kings Lynn Norfolk PE30 2QE
S9	A rural community at Syderstone of about 250 people employed in farming, but some from the professions or management who have retired. A large number of old people.	There is a 'native' population, about $2/3$ of the community, who are in social group V. The remaining $1/3$ of newcomers are in groups I to IV. Their main needs are for money, work and family stability. They think religion is irrelevant today.	'Native' population only about 2% Christian. Total population includes 10% committed Christians. There is a strong village Christian Fellowship and local Anglican, Baptist and Methodist churches.	Rev M Dilly 52 Tattersett Road Syderstone Kings Lynn Norfolk PE31 8SA
S10	150 to 200 mainly young adults living on an inner city housing development at Norwich. They are mainly employed in engineering, but there are some students.	Social groups III & IV. Concerned about isolation and unemployment. They have a non-Church culture where drug abuse and promiscuity are common.	7% are Christian. The Baptists and the Church of England are in contact.	Rev K Stewart St Mary's Manse Chester Place Norwich NR2 3DG
S11	60 or more men and women on a council estate at Ashill. Mixed ages and working in factories or as farm labourers.	Social group IV. Concerned with material things and apathetic regarding the Gospel.	9% Christian. There is occasional visiting by the Anglican church.	Mrs D Mellows The Rectory Ashill Norfolk IP25 7BT
S12	1,000 people living at Newton Flotman. They loosely identify with the village and are generally self-contained. Mixture of ages. Most work in Norwich, many in insurance or mustard manufacture.	Social groups I, II & III. They are rather materialistic but they do have a folk religion.	5% Christian. There is outreach from the local Anglican church.	Rev L Grimwade The Rectory 4 Dell Close Newton Flotman Norwich NR15 1RG

ETHNIC/LINGUISTIC GROUPS

	Description & Location	Characteristics	Openings for Outreach	Contact Person
E1	Between 150 and 250 Muslims, both foreign and national. Many are students. Men and women of all ages.	Their origins are Middle Eastern. 95% can read English. The mother tongue is Arabic and the religion is Islam. They have their own mosque.	No Christians. There is no outreach.	Mr Les Stebbings Pocket Testament League 3 Lubbock Close Norwich NR2 3QY

OCCASIONAL GROUPS

	Description & Location	Characteristics	Openings for Outreach	Contact Person
O1	Various social groups, each of about 20-30 people who meet for activities at Middleton. Includes youth club, play group, sports clubs, over 60s. They usually meet weekly, and are all young except for over 60s. Housewives and men in various employment.	Social groups III & IV. They meet together to develop skills or for relaxation. Their habits of life keep them from contact with worshipping community.	3% Christians. Anglican church in most contact and vicar sees play-group mothers regularly.	Rev A Green Middleton Vicarage 12 Hall Orchards Middleton Kings Lynn PE32 1RY
O2	There are groups of young people around the council housing estates of Norwich. Most are at school or unemployed. They have various cults: skinheads, punks and glue sniffers. Both sexes.	All unskilled group. There is a need for identity and selfworth. Most need to be loved. There are not enough Christians interested in them.	No known Christians. There is outreach and counselling by an evangelist, but more work is needed among them.	Mr Les Stebbings Pocket Testament League 3 Lubbock Close Norwich NR2 3QY
O3	A group of 30 senior citizens of similar background. Some are local, some are retired. All members of The Good Friends Club at Docking. All over 60. Men and women meeting weekly.	Social group III. They have a need for friendship. They have had a lifetime of leaving Christ out of their lives.	19% Christian, but no church attenders. Church of England and the nonconformist church are in contact. They have a special service once a month.	Rev J F B Jowitt The Vicarage Docking Kings Lynn PE31 8PN
O4	Far East prisoners of war at Dereham. About 20 men who were imprisoned by the Japanese during the Second World War. All in older age group.	Problems are medical and psychological. Many are still angry with God and utterly disillusioned to know the depths to which human nature can sink.	No known Christians. There is a Norfolk Chaplain in contact.	n/a

NORTHAMPTONSHIRE

Total population:	537,000
Estimated number attending church:	49,000
Total number not regularly attending church:	**488,000**
Non-attenders as percentage of population:	91%

Number of people not regularly attending church:

Age		Sex	
Under 15:	117,000	**Men:**	244,000
15-19:	39,000	**Women:**	244,000
20-29:	78,000		
30-44:	93,000		
45-64:	102,000		
65 or over:	59,000		

SOCIAL/COMMUNITY GROUPS

	Description & Location	Characteristics	Openings for Outreach	Contact Person
S1	Between 10,000 and 20,000 people on a 1930s council housing estate at Northampton. Many old but the young marrieds are replacing them. Artisan employment: boot and shoe and light engineering.	Groups III, IV & V. Main worries are those resulting from low income and unemployment. There is no contact and no mission.	1% Christian. They need their own church and minister. The community now split between two Anglican parishes, neither properly staffed.	Rev F E Pickard 5 Abington Park Crescent Northampton NN3 3AD
S2	2,000 people living on two housing estates in isolation outside Northampton.	Social group III. Community focus is required.	2-3% Christian. There is limited visitation by the Baptists. No churches in the area.	Mr Stuart Jenkins The Manse West Street Moulton Northants NN3 1SB
S3	160 people living in adjacent roads on a new housing estate at Towcester. Varied non-manual employment including electronic engineering. Mainly young marrieds with children.	Social groups I, II & III. They want to be accepted and live in a friendly atmosphere. Too busy and self sufficient to be interested in Gospel.	5% Christian. Occasional leaflet drop and some door-to-door visitation. Church of England and Baptist in contact.	Mr & Mrs Oxley 14 Wordsworth Close Towcester Northants NN12 7JU
S4	About 30 families living at Grimscote, engaged in farming or professional work. Many old and young people.	Social groups I, II & III. Materialism and apostacy keep them from Christianity.	6% Christian. The Baptist church are attempting outreach. Anglicans also in contact.	Mr R G Barr 20 Chipsey Avenue Bugbrooke Northants NN7 3QW

	Description & Location	Characteristics	Openings for Outreach	Contact Person
S5	600 people working at Plesseys Research Centre near Towcester. Mainly young marrieds.	Professional and management. Their main concern is success and a high salary. They are highly qualified and some have a feeling of superiority.	3% Christian. Church of England, Baptist, Methodist and Roman Catholic churches all have contact.	n/a

OCCASIONAL GROUPS

	Description & Location	Characteristics	Openings for Outreach	Contact Person
O1	Up to 30 young people of both sexes, mostly unemployed, who attend a coffee bar at Emmanuel Shared Church at Weston Favell.	Unskilled social group. There is a need to understand how these young people feel about themselves. They feel that the Church is quite foreign to them.	The number of Christians is not known. All denominations are represented by local shared church who are attempting outreach.	Rev N Beattie Emmanuel Shared Church Weston Favell Northampton NN3 4JR
O2	At Wellingborough a group of 30 young mothers with toddlers. They are housewives whose husbands work in factories.	Semi-skilled and unskilled groups. Mixed races. Not enough care shown to them by churches.	5% Christian. They meet in URC Community building. Anglican minister calls monthly.	Rev H Smart All Saints Vicarage 18 Midland Road Wellingborough Northants NN8 1NF

NORTHUMBERLAND

Total population:	300,000
Estimated number attending church:	26,000
Total number not regularly attending church:	**274,000**
Non-attenders as percentage of population:	91%

Number of people not regularly attending church:

Age		Sex	
Under 15:	58,000	Men:	134,000
15-19:	22,000	Women:	140,000
20-29:	38,000		
30-44:	49,000		
45-64:	66,000		
65 or over:	41,000		

SOCIAL/COMMUNITY GROUPS

	Description & Location	Characteristics	Openings for Outreach	Contact Person
S1	3,000 people in a coal mining community at Alnwick. Most of the men are working in the coal industry. Some of the women work as cleaners or shop workers. Mixed ages.	Social groups III, IV and V. A male-dominated society. Most evenings are spent in social clubs. Church is thought of as for women and old people.	1% Christian. The Anglican church is 1½ miles away, and there is no outreach apart from a youth club.	Mr J G Tweeddale 3 Hillcrest Park Alnwick Northumberland NE66 2NW
S2	3,000 people living on council estates at Hexham. Working as caretakers, drivers, labourers etc. Many old and young people.	Social groups III, IV and V. There is a huge credibility gap and the Church seems irrelevant to them.	5% Christian. The Salvation Army sometimes visits. There is no church in the area.	Mr Eric Wright Westfield Westfield Terrace Hexham Northumberland NE46 3DJ

Total population:	678,000
Estimated number attending church:	65,000
Total number not regularly attending church:	**613,000**
Non-attenders as percentage of population:	90%

Number of people not regularly attending church:

Age		Sex	
Under 15:	129,000	**Men:**	300,000
15-19:	49,000	**Women:**	313,000
20-29:	86,000		
30-44:	110,000		
45-64:	141,000		
65 or over:	98,000		

SOCIAL/COMMUNITY GROUPS

	Description & Location	Characteristics	Openings for Outreach	Contact Person
S1	A group of 17,500 in rural north Yorkshire, in an area of nine churches. Mostly young adults, working in offices or mining.	Social class III and IV. Concerned about youth problems and unemployment. Poor discipleship and apathy even among church attenders.	25% Christian. RC, Anglican and Methodist contact.	Rev M W Calver 24 Tomlinson Way Sherburn-in-Elmet Leeds LS25 6EQ
S2	300 to 400 at Northallerton living on a council estate. Mostly men, young and middle aged. Farm and other manual workers, many unemployed.	Social class IV and V. Worried about money and unemployment. They consider the Church irrelevant.	No known Christians. All churches are in the area and all have contact. There is a Pentecostal Youth Club.	n/a
S3	Elderly people living in flats and bungalows in Huntington. Retired manual workers.	Social class III and IV. They are well served socially and physically. There is indifference to the Church and many are housebound.	About 20% Christian. Methodist, Anglican, RC, and Salvation Army contact.	n/a
S4	4,000 on a council estate near the centre of Scarborough. Residents mainly employed in shops. Mixed age range.	Social class III, IV and V. Conscious of financial problems. They have preconceived ideas about church going.	1% Christian. Anglican and Pentecostal contact.	Mr Neal Stephenson 146 Barrowcliff Road Scarborough N Yorks YO12 6EY
S5	1,500, mostly young families, living on a private estate near Northallerton. Management and clerical workers, mostly for local council.	Social class I, II and III. Under increasing stress from fear of redundancy.	7% Christian. Anglican and Methodist contact.	Rev M Stopford The Manse 21 Helmsley Way Northallerton N Yorks OC7 8TA

ETHNIC/LINGUISTIC GROUPS

Description & Location	Characteristics	Openings for Outreach	Contact Person
E1 A group of 40 Filipino workers employed in hotels in Scarborough.	70% read English. Mother tongue is Ilocano; religion is Roman Catholic. They feel isolated, and their attitude to religion is often very superstitious.	No known contact.	Mr Neal Stephenson 146 Barrowcliff Road Scarborough N Yorks YO12 6EY

OCCASIONAL GROUPS

Description & Location	Characteristics	Openings for Outreach	Contact Person
O1 About 100 meeting for outdoor activities. Majority older men and women.	Social class II and III. Consider that the Church is irrelevant.	Number of Christians not known. Anglican contact.	Rev Ronald Atkinson 13 Lawn Way Stockton Lane York YO3 0JN
O2 300 members of a Working Men's Club at Norton. Mostly factory and steel workers.	Social class III and IV. They see the church as middle-class. They have a vague idea that all will be all right in the end.	2% Christian. Limited Anglican contact.	Rev D B Cooper Norton Vicarage Malton N Yorks YO17 9AE
O3 About 1,500 soldiers and families in MOD housing at Ripon. Many children.	Social class III and IV. Main concern is separation from family because they are constantly moving. This also means they seldom settle in a church.	Very few Christians. Anglican, Methodist and RC contact. The Padre holds pastoral outreach and services.	Rev R B B Wild Trinity Vicarage Ripon N Yorks HG4 2AE
O4 About 50 members of a friendship club in Halifax, meeting on Methodist premises. Mainly retired.	Social class III and IV. Many are lonely. They are largely apathetic to the church, not knowing what it is like today.	60% Christian. Club leaders are Christian.	n/a
O5 A group of 500 CB enthusiasts in the Scarborough area. Mainly young and many unemployed.	Social class V. Their main need is for jobs. The church has not been clearly presented to them.	Very few Christians. No known contact. Contact could be made through CB.	Mr Neal Stephenson 146 Barrowcliff Road Scarborough N Yorks YO12 6EY
O6 About 100 members of a group in York who raise money for good causes.	Social class I and II. They meet to serve the needs of others. They have no vital experience of the Gospel.	5% Christian. Anglican contact.	Rev R Atkinson 13 Lawn Way Stockton Lane York YO3 0JD
O7 About 60 members of Mother and Toddler groups in Halifax, meeting on Methodist premises. Young mothers and their children.	Social class III and IV. Many feel isolated, having left work to bring up a family.	10% Christian. Anglican contact.	n/a

Total population:	991,000
Estimated number attending church:	61,000
Total number not regularly attending church:	**930,000**
Non-attenders as percentage of population:	94%

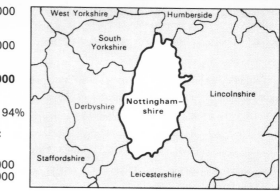

Number of people not regularly attending church:

Age		Sex	
Under 15:	205,000	**Men:**	456,000
15-19:	74,000	**Women:**	474,000
20-29:	130,000		
30-44:	177,000		
45-64:	214,000		
65 or over:	130,000		

SOCIAL/COMMUNITY GROUPS

	Description & Location	Characteristics	Openings for Outreach	Contact Person
S1	A parish of 22,000 people near the city centre in Nottingham. Council house tenants or first time buyers. There is much unemployment. The workers are in factories. Originally a lot of old people but now more younger ones moving in.	Social group IV and V. All need a pastoral caring ministry. They see God as irrelevant to their lives.	1% Christian. There are Methodists, Baptists, Roman Catholics, Church of England and Seventh Day Adventists in contact, and there is some outreach.	Rev J P Neill The Vicarage 17 Robin Hood Chase St Ann's Nottingham NG3 4EY
S2	6,000 people on new estates near the village of Calverton. Mostly a mining community plus newcomers, both young and just retiring. Employed in the coal industry. There are also some teachers.	Social groups III and IV. Concerned with security and education. They have outgrown the faith of the 'family' church from which they came.	About 1% Christian. Contact through Mission England and the free churches. There are Church of England, Methodist, Baptist and Pentecostal churches.	n/a
S3	A housing estate to the north of Nottingham with a population of 10,000. Both young and old. Employed largely in the coal industry or unemployed.	Social groups III, IV and V. Needs are mainly pastoral in a disadvantaged area. There is a secular group consciousness which excludes the Church. People are much concerned with their own problems.	Under 2% Christian. Denominations in contact are the ecumenical Anglican/ Methodist church, the Roman Catholics and Assemblies of God.	Mr Ted Lyons 36 Melksham Road Bestwood Park Nottingham NG5 5RX
S4	A socially deprived council estate of 10,000 people. Employed as labourers. Large numbers of old and young people.	Unskilled, their main concern is having enough to live on. They have difficulty understanding spiritual concepts. They have so many problems simply coping with life.	4% Christian. There is outreach in evangelistic services, Sunday Schools and youth work. There is a Pentecostal church and Church of England.	Mr John Parker 44 Apollo Drive Hempshill Vale Nottingham NG6 7AF

	Description & Location	Characteristics	Openings for Outreach	Contact Person
S5	10 to 20 old men and women in sheltered accommodation for the elderly in Nottingham.	All need care and someone to talk to.	3% Christian. Anglicans, Methodists and Baptists in contact, and outreach is being undertaken.	n/a
S6	2,000 people living on a post-war residential development of private houses at W Bridgford. A growing number of older couples with white collar jobs. Some wives are employed in offices and shops.	Social groups II and III. They are concerned with finance and job security, and have traditional ideas of morality, religion and Church.	15% Christian. Outreach through the local Council of Churches, visitation with Gospels, and contact with local Church of England.	n/a

ETHNIC/LINGUISTIC GROUPS

	Description & Location	Characteristics	Openings for Outreach	Contact Person
E1	2,000 Chinese people and Vietnam refugees, from Hong Kong and Vietnam. They work mostly in restaurants or take-aways, and a few are in industry. Men and women of all ages.	5 to 10% read English. Their mother tongue is Cantonese and they are normally Buddhists. They lead busy lives and have little time for religion. Their own culture is non-Christian.	4% Christian. There is a Chinese Fellowship and the Chinese Overseas Christian Mission attempts outreach.	Mr Marcus Stone 12 Cavendish Avenue Gedling Nottingham NG4 4FZ

OCCASIONAL GROUPS

	Description & Location	Characteristics	Openings for Outreach	Contact Person
O1	A youth club at Beeston with 60 members. Most are at school or unemployed. Both sexes, meeting weekly.	Social groups of the families are III and IV. Main need is for somewhere to go to get off the streets. They are apathetic towards the Gospel or put off by the way it has been presented to them.	5% Christian. Outreach through MAYC. Methodist Church has most contact. There is a need for counselling on youth problems, especially glue sniffing.	Rev F R Ireland 39 Bramcote Drive Beeston Nottingham NG9 1AT
O2	70 teachers at a comprehensive school in Nottingham. Men and women of various ages.	Their main concern is for financial and job security, job satisfaction and family success. Humanistic training and materialistic, cynical outlook on life keeps them from the Gospel.	10% Christian. Anglican and Baptist churches have most contact but there is no outreach.	n/a
O3	50 members of a tennis club at Sutton-in-Ashfield. Aged between 18 and 45, but a few older. Men and women. They are employed in education, insurance, selling, fire service.	Social groups II and III. Their needs are material. They are conscious of poverty etc around the world and social issues, but there is little contact with committed Christians.	6% Christian. The Church of England and Methodist church have contact.	n/a

Description & Location	Characteristics	Openings for Outreach	Contact Person
O4 A Mother and Toddler group at Kirkby in Ashfield with 50 members meeting weekly. Working as shop assistants and factory work; their husbands are usually miners. All young women.	Social group IV. Concerned with material needs in their own community. Their attitude is that religion is irrelevant.	10% Christian. There is need for support through friendship and contact at home. No outreach specifically to this group. Anglicans and Methodists have most contact.	Rev G Etheridge 24 Pearl Avenue Kirkby in Ashfield Nottinghamshire NG17 7FE

OXFORDSHIRE

Total population:	548,000
Estimated number attending church:	47,000
Total number not regularly attending church:	**501,000**
Non-attenders as percentage of population:	91%

Number of people not regularly attending church:

Age		Sex	
Under 15:	106,000	**Men:**	266,000
15-19:	45,000	**Women:**	235,000
20-29:	85,000		
30-44:	105,000		
45-64:	100,000		
65 or over:	60,000		

SOCIAL/COMMUNITY GROUPS

	Description & Location	Characteristics	Openings for Outreach	Contact Person
S1	2,000 population of the village of Bampton. Full age range, mostly computing professionals employed in the University, accountancy and law. Some manual workers and unemployed.	All social groups included, but most are professional. They are very conscious of financial matters and see Jesus Christ as irrelevant, if not fictional.	5% Christian. The Church of England has slight contact.	n/a
S2	500 on a council estate in Oxford. All ages and almost no employment for the unskilled population. Some are employed in factories.	Social group V. All are worried about employment. Moral laxity and indifference keep them from God.	No known Christians. The Baptist Church are attempting outreach with door-to-door visiting, children's work etc.	Mr Nigel Soper 37 Lytton Road Oxford OX4 3PA
S3	A group of about 80 adults in young families living in a council housing development of flats in Abingdon centre. Most are employed on assembly lines on the industrial estate.	Semi skilled workers with money worries. Their experience of church-goers alienates them from the Gospel.	Perhaps 12% nominal Anglicans. Outreach through Abingdon Council of Churches.	n/a
S4	3,000 factory workers at Cowley, mostly men and many West Indians working as fitters and assemblers etc. Mixed ages.	Social groups III and IV. There is a great need for them to break from the monotony of factory work. Most are hardened men who see religion as soft.	10% Christian. West Indian Pentecostal Churches have strong contacts and there is a Christian Society at British Leyland.	Mr L Pavey 20 Great Close Road Yarnton Oxon OX5 1QW

	Description & Location	Characteristics	Openings for Outreach	Contact Person
S5	1,000 lecturers, fellows and tutors at Oxford University. Men and women, mainly middle-aged.	All are professional group I. Conscious of academic knowledge, social standing and academic achievement. Pride and ignorance of real Christianity keep them from the Gospel.	5% Christian. There is door-to-door visitation, guest services and special meetings.	Mr Nigel Soper 37 Lytton Road Oxford OX4 3PA
S6	3,500 people in the expanded village of Bloxham, now four times its original size. There is a predominance of younger people mostly in executive positions in marketing, banking, schools etc.	Social group II. Main concern is the family and bringing up their children. There is a feeling that religion is irrelevant to the 'self made' man, and that the Christian Church does not greatly care about them.	3% Christian. There are Baptist, Anglican and Roman Catholic churches, and the Baptists are attempting outreach.	Rev John Goddard 27 Lawrence Leys Bloxham Banbury Oxon OX15 4NU
S7	The children in the four schools at Bloxham. 700 in two public schools, 1,000 in the comprehensive and 400 in the primary.	There is scepticism about the churches and Christianity, and they are alienated from the adult population.	It is difficult to estimate the number of Christians. There is no organised outreach, and no youth club in village.	Rev John Goddard 27 Lawrence Leys Bloxham Banbury Oxon OX15 4NU

OCCASIONAL GROUPS

O1	A group of about 200 drifters, glue sniffers, drug abusers and alcoholics who congregate in the city of Oxford. Mainly young people of both sexes. The majority are unemployed.	Unskilled people whose problems are physical and emotional. Life holds no hope for them and they see no way out.	5% Christian. Outreach through Teen Challenge Oxford. There are Anglican and Pentecostal churches.	Mr L Pavey 20 Great Close Road Yarnton Oxon OX5 1QW
O2	About 20 young men and women in a gang of 'punks' who gather in public places in Bicester. All are unemployed.	Social group V. They lack money, jobs, acceptance, love. A culture gap divides them from the Church.	No known Christians. One or two people from Methodist Church are seeking to befriend them.	Mr J S Kyle 34 Banbury Road Bicester Oxon OX6 7NH

SHROPSHIRE

Total population:	380,000
Estimated number attending church:	32,000
Total number not regularly attending church:	**348,000**
Non-attenders as percentage of population:	92%

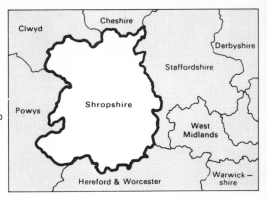

Number of people not regularly attending church:

Age		Sex	
Under 15:	77,000	**Men:**	171,000
15-19:	28,000	**Women:**	177,000
20-29:	49,000		
30-44:	66,000		
45-64:	76,000		
65 or over:	52,000		

SOCIAL/COMMUNITY GROUPS

	Description & Location	Characteristics	Openings for Outreach	Contact Person
S1	500 residents of a council estate at Market Drayton, considered a problem area. Men and women employed in factories or labouring. All ages.	Unskilled, suffering financial hardship and from the bad reputation of the area. Thought to be unsympathetic to Christianity but they have shown enthusiasm for carol singers etc.	Number of Christians not known. No local church.	Rev R Swain Wesley House 1 Clive Road Market Drayton Shropshire TF9 3DJ
S2	150 people living in council houses in a 'county' area at Porthywaen. Much unemployment, but some work in quarry. Men and women of all ages.	Social groups IV and V. The local church is very middle-class and they feel they do not belong.	10% Christian. The nearest church is two miles away. Outreach by Rev Peter Gledhill.	Rev P Gledhill The Vicarage Oswestry Shropshire SY10 8NO

Total population: 432,000

Estimated number attending church: 43,000

Total number not regularly attending church: 389,000

Non-attenders as percentage of population: 90%

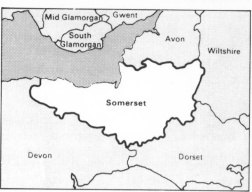

Number of people not regularly attending church:

Age		Sex	
Under 15:	78,000	**Men:**	195,000
15-19:	31,000	**Women:**	194,000
20-29:	58,000		
30-44:	74,000		
45-64:	90,000		
65 or over:	58,000		

SOCIAL/COMMUNITY GROUPS

	Description & Location	Characteristics	Openings for Outreach	Contact Person
S1	About 100 landowners with labourers in attendance plus retired service officers and businessmen settled in the country around Bruton. Mostly older people. Men and women.	Social classes I and II apart from the labourers, who are skilled and semi-skilled manual workers. Self-interest keeps them from the Good News.	5% Christian. The local Council of Churches and the Anglicans attempt outreach.	Rev C Atkin Pitcombe Rectory Bruton Somerset BA10 0PE
S2	The village of Stogumber. About 100 wealthy retired people in their own homes; about 60 council tenants; 50 elderly people in council bungalows, 50 'natives'. Men and women. Predominantly old.	Social groups I, III and IV. There is a lack of visible Christian witness for them to associate with.	Under 1% Christian. The Church of England and the Baptists are in contact.	Mr Peter Wilson The Baptist Manse Stogumber Somerset TA43 3SZ

OCCASIONAL GROUPS

O1	A group of 30 young mothers who meet at a pre-school playgroup in a church hall at Yeovil. All housewives.	The husbands are in social group III. Their main concern is with child care. They have no conscious need for the Gospel.	No Christians. The Church of England and Elim have contact. Some need spiritual help and support while naval husbands are at sea. Some outreach through church coffee mornings.	Mr G Holmes 15 Stiby Road Yeovil Somerset BA21 3EE
O2	A local social group at Taunton with 40 members. All women aged between 40 and 70. Mainly housewives with some in part time or voluntary work. (See note.)	Social group III. Their main problem is loneliness. There is a lack of awareness of any need for the Gospel.	Most are nominally Christian but 10%-15% have an active interest. One or two Christians in the group attempt outreach, supported by vicar.	n/a

SOUTH YORKSHIRE

Total population: 1,313,000

Estimated number
attending church: 79,000

**Total number not regularly
attending church: 1,234,000**

Non-attenders as
percentage of population: 94%

Number of people not regularly attending church:

Age		Sex	
Under 15:	271,000	**Men:**	605,000
15-19:	99,000	**Women:**	629,000
20-29:	173,000		
30-44:	222,000		
45-64:	296,000		
65 or over:	173,000		

SOCIAL/COMMUNITY GROUPS

	Description & Location	Characteristics	Openings for Outreach	Contact Person
S1	About 300 people living on two small council estates in a village near Sheffield. Manual workers of mixed ages.	Social class III, IV and V. Financial needs are the greatest problem. There is a lack of communication with the Church.	1% Christian. Anglican contact.	n/a
S2	2,000 in a pit village near Rotherham, all ages, mostly employed in the colliery or the steel works. A number are now redundant.	Social class III and IV. Main concern is job security. The Christian tradition seems irrelevant to working classes. Village churches have very limited resources.	Number of Christians not known. Anglican, Baptist and Methodist contact.	n/a
S3	Hundreds of members of Working Men's Clubs around Barnsley. All ages; most employed in coal mining.	Social class III, IV and V. Main concerns are money, job security and recreation. Working Men's Clubs form a close-knit community and satisfying lifestyle. Christianity is irrelevant.	Number of Christians not known.	Mr M Dennison 173 Park Grove Barnsley S70 1QY
S4	A group of 300 living on a housing estate in Sheffield. Mostly young families. Mostly manual steel workers, but many unemployed.	Social class III. Problems of unemployment and resentment of young people. The churches seem to try to maintain the village community, excluding outsiders.	3% Christian. Some visiting and work with children, by Anglican, Pentecostal and Methodist.	Rev R J Buckley Woodhouse Vicarage Barn Lane Sheffield S13 7LL
S5	5,000 on an estate in Darnall with some privately owned houses. Many older people, employed in steel industry.	Social class III, IV and V. They lack conscious spiritual need. The Gospel has not been communicated in a way they understand.	3% Christian. No known outreach. Pentecostal, Anglican, Methodist, RC, and Salvation Army in the area.	n/a

Description & Location	Characteristics	Openings for Outreach	Contact Person
S6 1,000 on a council estate in Sheffield. Mostly older people employed in industry.	Social class IV and V. They suffer from loneliness, powerless-ness and frustration. They feel alienated from the class and culture of churchgoers.	10% Christian. Joint events planned by the local Council of Churches. Door-to-door visitation by Baptists.	Mr Malcolm Carroll 32 Southview Crescent Sheffield S7 1DM
S7 50 young families living in older housing in Sheffield.	Social class IV. Need establishment of community relationships. Many are indifferent to the Church, though much goodwill towards it.	5% Christian. Methodist contact.	Rev E M Marriott 4 Derriman Close Sheffield S11 9LB
S8 A group of 2,500 mining families living largely in NCB housing at Armthorpe.	Social class III and IV. Their needs are materialistic, family and money. Simple unbelief, and folk religion keep them from the Gospel.	Less than 1% Christian. Historically they were Methodists but not today. There are churches in the area.	Rev John Peek Armthorpe Rectory Armthorpe Doncaster DN3 3ID

ETHNIC/LINGUISTIC GROUPS

Description & Location	Characteristics	Openings for Outreach	Contact Person
E1 A group of many hundreds from Pakistan and the Near East, who mostly work in the steelworks at Sheffield. Mainly living in poor housing.	10% read English easily. Mother tongues are Urdu or Arabic; religion is Islam.	Local churches support a Christian from Pakistan who works among them, as evangelist and teacher.	n/a
E2 2,000 from Pakistan. Many children. Men work in transport, industry and shops; high unemployment. They live in the poorer part of Tinsley.	60% read English. Mother tongue is Urdu (written) and Punjabi (spoken); religion is Islam. They come from a country district and their culture and relationships bind them to Islam.	DATIC of Sheffield has a worker with his family in the area.	Rev H W Everest St Lawrence Vicarage 24 Highgate Tinsley Sheffield S9 1WL
E3 2,000 mainly rural Pakistanis living in Burngreave, Darnall and Abbeydale in the Sheffield area. They work in shops and steel works.	50% read English. Mother tongue is Urdu; religion is Islam. There is a cultural tightness and solidarity in the community.	No known Christians. There is an Asian Christian worker.	Mr John Smith 4 Thornsett Road Sheffield S7 1NA

OCCASIONAL GROUPS

Description & Location	Characteristics	Openings for Outreach	Contact Person
O1 50 members of an Over 60s afternoon group at Conisbrough.	Social class III and IV. Their main concern is loneliness. There is an ingrained misunder-standing of the Gospel.	12% Christian. Baptist and Anglican contact.	Mr D M Newton 24A Old Road Conisbrough Doncaster DN12 3NB

Description & Location	Characteristics	Openings for Outreach	Contact Person
O2 Young people in the working-class area of Crookes, Sheffield, meeting at the Crookes Youth Centre every week. Many unemployed.	Social class III and IV. Many are put off church by condemnatory attitude of Christians. Their concerns are lacking money, resources and caring helpers.	10% Christian. The Anglican and Baptist joint church is in contact. There are church youth workers as volunteers.	Mr S J Williams Crookes Endowed Centre Crookes Road Sheffield S10 1UB
O3 60 members of Mother and Toddler group in Rossington. Husbands mainly miners.	Social class III and IV. Apathetic about Gospel and think it irrelevant.	6% Christian. Pentecostal contact.	Mr D A Jones 38 Windsor Road Town Moor Doncaster DN2 5BT

Total population: 1,019,000

Estimated number
attending church: 78,000

**Total number not regularly
attending church: 941,000**

Non-attenders as
percentage of population: 92%

Number of people not regularly attending church:

Age		Sex	
Under 15:	217,000	**Men:**	461,000
15-19:	75,000	**Women:**	480,000
20-29:	141,000		
30-44:	188,000		
45-64:	217,000		
65 or over:	103,000		

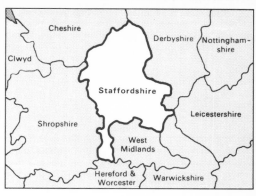

SOCIAL/COMMUNITY GROUPS

	Description & Location	Characteristics	Openings for Outreach	Contact Person
S1	4,000 to 5,000 people living on a council estate at Lichfield. Young people and young to middle-aged marrieds with children. All working class on low incomes or unemployed. Those working are in factories, offices or shops.	Social groups IV and V. There is a need for counselling on marriage and family life. They are concerned with material needs and have religious misconceptions of Church.	2% Christian. The Pentecostal church and the Church of England involved in outreach. There are also Methodists and Roman Catholics in contact.	Mr John T Wyre 25 Southwark Close Lichfield Staffs WS13 7SH
S2	10,000 people living in the north of Stafford, in mostly Victorian terraced houses and council houses. A few on private estates. Most of them work in factories. Some of the private house dwellers are in professional or management work.	Most are semi-skilled. Main concerns are to do with money and unemployment. There is a lack of knowledge of God, not helped by lack of local witness.	Less than 1% are Christian. There is a group seeking to establish an evangelical church. There is an Anglo-Catholic church in the area.	Mr T Irwin 11 Cooperative Street Stafford ST16 3BZ
S3	23,000 people on a council housing estate outside Hanley, Stoke on Trent. Many young people. Many are unemployed and the others work in pottery or mining.	Social groups IV and V. They are only vaguely aware that the churches exist, and do not see any relevance in them.	1% Christian. Church of England, Roman Catholic and Methodist churches on estate.	Mr M E Stafford 120 Winchester Avenue Bentilee Stoke-on-Trent ST2 0LP
S4	1,400 men and women living at Mayfield. 60% in council houses. Very varied employment and mix of ages.	Social grades III and IV. There is a pub-centred culture, and a sense of satisfaction with themselves, even among the children.	2% Christian. The Church of England and the Methodists have contact, and work specifically among the children and the over 60s.	Rev D Service Mayfield Vicarage Ashbourne Staffs DE6 2JR

	Description & Location	Characteristics	Openings for Outreach	Contact Person
S5	800 to 1,000 people living on a council estate at Kidsgrove. Most moved from mining villages of Durham in the 60s. Many are now unemployed, the local mines having closed.	Social groups III, IV and V. They feel self-sufficient and not conscious of any spiritual needs. They seem to resent any approach by the churches.	1% Christian. There are Methodist, Roman Catholic and Anglican churches in the area.	Rev C Topping 'Coniston' The Avenue Kidsgrove Stoke-on-Trent ST7 1AQ

ETHNIC/LINGUISTIC GROUPS

E1	60 or 70 men and women from Pakistan living at Longton. Have formed a small community with their own shops, taxis milkman etc. Many young people.	70% can read English easily. Their religion is Islam and they have their own mosque.	No Christians and no outreach.	Mr Terry Barlow 123 Chaplin Road Longton Staffs ST3 4RT

OCCASIONAL GROUPS

O1	A youth club at Stafford, with 50 members of both sexes. Mostly at school.	Conscious of their own social needs and consider the news of Christ irrelevant.	5% Christian. The Methodist church is involved with them.	Mr G S Hall 5 Widecombe Ave Weeping Cross Stafford ST17 0HX

Total population: 611,000

Estimated number
attending church: 59,000

**Total number not regularly
attending church: 552,000**

Non-attenders as
percentage of population: 90%

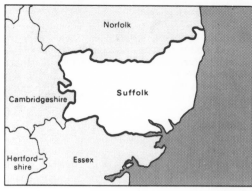

Number of people not regularly attending church:

Age		Sex	
Under 15:	116,000	**Men:**	276,000
15-19:	39,000	**Women:**	276,000
20-29:	83,000		
30-44:	110,000		
45-64:	121,000		
65 or over:	83,000		

SOCIAL/COMMUNITY GROUPS

	Description & Location	Characteristics	Openings for Outreach	Contact Person
S1	400 homes in an area of Ipswich formed into a community association. Mostly young people, engaged in dock work or light engineering.	Social groups IV and V. Conscious of social and material needs, with a wish to upgrade the community. Established church worship. The Baptists had a church; the people came and then left.	Number of Christians not known. There is visitation and nurture groups plus a youth club. There is no church in the area.	Rev D Meikle St Matthew's Rectory Prescott Road Ipswich IP1 2EX
S2	A group of 1,000 indigenous inhabitants of Saxmundham. Older people and some families. Employed in service industries and local light industry.	Semi-skilled workers whose problem is that they are not conscious of any need, and look upon themselves as self-sufficient.	1% Christian. There is outreach from the Anglican church in visiting etc. URC also in area.	Rev H Boreham The Rectory Manor Gardens Saxmundham Suffolk IP17 1ET
S3	40 residents in a street in the dormitory village of Sproughton. All council property. Men and women of all ages, employed as labourers, drivers, shop assistants etc.	Social groups IV and V. They are not conscious of any needs. They see the Church as not being for people of their class.	No Christians. There is ordinary parish contact, with the rector visiting.	Rev N Clarke Sproughton Rectory Sproughton Suffolk IP8 3BQ
S4	500 people living in five small villages around Bungay, employed in farming and local industries. No special age group. Men and women.	Social groups III and IV. They have a need for stability, and a desire to be left alone. There has been a previous lack of evangelism from the Church.	No known Christians. There is an Anglican church in contact and outreach is undertaken by the rector of Flixton.	Rev P A Skoulding Flixton Rectory Bungay Suffolk NR35 1NL

	Description & Location	Characteristics	Openings for Outreach	Contact Person
S5	1,000 residents of a small private housing estate near Stowmarket. They are either retired or working for ICI, on RAF bases, for the Civil Service or British Telecom. There are also some teachers and self-employed. More old people than average, but also some young families.	Social groups II, III, and IV. Those who are retired want a quiet and happy retirement. The younger ones want to move to larger houses etc. There is a lack of effective Christian witness in the area.	Up to 15% churchgoers but less than 10% Christian. The Church of England and the URC visit.	Rev David Mathers Old Newton Vicarage Stowmarket Suffolk IP14 4HF

ETHNIC/LINGUISTIC GROUPS

	Description & Location	Characteristics	Openings for Outreach	Contact Person
O1	25 to 30 Vietnamese Boat People from North Vietnam in a block of maisonettes at Felixstowe. Mainly unemployed, but two work in a Chinese restaurant and some have seasonal work in hotels. Men and women and large number of children and teenagers.	20% can read English, but this is mainly the teenagers. Their mother tongue is Vietnamese or Chinese. No personal religion but their background is Buddhist. Language is a barrier, and the older people are shy in their relationships with British people.	No Christians, but two of the younger teenagers have shown interest. There are two Christian voluntary workers and a Christian teacher of English.	Mrs Sheila Rivers St Kilda Falcon Street Felixstowe IP11 9DR
E2	A group of American Air Force servicemen and their families, living in 150 houses at Saxmundham. Mainly young.	95% can read English easily; it is their mother tongue. Families usually stay for three or four years. Many are prejudiced from their experiences of American religious sects and cults.	2% Christian. They are treated as part of the parish. There is a USAF Chaplain on the base, 10 miles away.	Rev H Boreham The Rectory Manor Gardens Saxmundham Suffolk IP17 1ET

OCCASIONAL GROUPS

	Description & Location	Characteristics	Openings for Outreach	Contact Person
O1	Large numbers of holiday-makers spending holidays or weekends on caravan sites and in holiday camps on the coast at Lowestoft and area.	Wide variety of social groups. There is a general lack of interest in the Church.	It is suggested that a low key approach through friendly contacts is best. There is a Norwich Diocesan holiday Chaplaincy and outreach through Holiday Clubs etc.	Capt David Sanderson 596 London Road Lowestoft Suffolk WR3 0LF
O2	A village youth club in Bures. Members drawn mainly from council and commuter estates. The numbers averaged 70+ meeting weekly. All young people of both sexes, working in factories, shops or nursing or still at school.	Social group III. Their main needs are social. Majority have no interest in the Gospel.	5% are Christian. The Church of England is in contact. There is contact between the few Christians and their friends. There are links between the active youth fellowship in the church and the members of the youth club.	Rev C D G Patterson The Vicarage Bures Suffolk CO8 5AA

Description & Location	Characteristics	Openings for Outreach	Contact Person
O3 A branch of the British Legion in Brandon with 250 members of all age groups, mostly labourers or unemployed. Men and women.	Unskilled people whose main need is making more money. Apathetic about the Gospel.	5% Christian. The president is a Christian as are some of the women.	n/a

SURREY

Total population: 1,014,000

Estimated number
attending church: 95,000

**Total number not regularly
attending church: 919,000**

Non-attenders as
percentage of population: 91%

Number of people not regularly attending church:

Age		Sex	
Under 15:	193,000	**Men:**	450,000
15-19:	73,000	**Women:**	469,000
20-29:	129,000		
30-44:	165,000		
45-64:	221,000		
65 or over:	138,000		

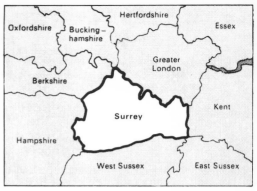

SOCIAL/COMMUNITY GROUPS

	Description & Location	Characteristics	Openings for Outreach	Contact Person
S1	2,000 tenants on a council estate at Surbiton. The normal age range.	Semi-skilled workers mainly concerned with economic needs. Unwilling to accept the priorities of the Kingdom of God. They see faith as irrelevant.	5% Christian. There is regular visiting and youth work. Anglican and Methodist churches have contact.	Rev David Smith 24 Alexandra Drive Surbiton Surrey KT5 9AB
S2	A group of 30 old people, all retired women, living at Addiscombe, Croydon.	All feel lonely and rejected. Most are open to receiving Christ but some have fear of a commitment.	25% Christian. There is contact with the Baptist church.	Mrs Pat Turner 164 Davidson Road Croydon Surrey CR0 6DE
S3	2,000 people in garden suburbs of Shirley. All in the higher income bracket earning their livings as high calibre salesmen, high technology boffins, accountants, stock brokers etc. Normal age range.	Social groups I, II and III. There is a lack of spiritual awareness and little contact with Christianity. Their material self-sufficiency is also a block to the Gospel.	Some nominal Christians. The Anglican church has most contact, but there is no outreach.	Miss Mitty Chattertee 28 Darley Close Shirley Croydon Surrey CR0 7QH
S4	1,000 men and women living in flats and bed-sits in Guildford town centre. Many are old and many types of employment are represented.	Social groups III and IV. The churches seem irrelevant to them. They are only used for weddings and funerals.	2% Christian. The Anglican, Methodist and Baptist churches are all in contact, and there is some visitation.	Mr Adrian Smith 8 Eastgate Gardens Guildford Surrey GU1 4AZ

	Description & Location	Characteristics	Openings for Outreach	Contact Person
S5	About 2,000 to 3,000 people in council houses and the poorer areas of Dorking. They spend their spare time in pubs or watching television or in each other's homes. Slightly more younger people, and a variety of employment.	Social groups III, IV and V. Their main concerns are health and money. The proclamation of the Gospel is irrelevant to their needs. They find it difficult to fit in with our 'respectable' churches.	Less than 1% Christian. There is outreach by the Elim and FIEC churches and visitation by the town missioner.	Mr John Le Boutillier 41 Hampstead Road Dorking Surrey RH4 3AE
S6	A large number of elderly people living alone in and around Farnham. More women than men. All retired.	Social groups I and II. Their main problems are loneliness and their lack of mobility. There is a great need for genuine friendship. They feel that no-one cares.	10 to 15% Christian. All denominations are in contact and there is visitation and help with transport.	Mr Kenneth Smith 45 Broomleaf Road Farnham Surrey GU9 8DZ
S7	2,500 people living on a fairly new estate to the east of Croydon. Working in clerical, administrative and professional employment. Men and women of all ages.	Social groups I, II and III. They are not conscious of any needs and self-satisfaction is a bar to the Gospel.	4% Christian. No known outreach.	n/a
S8	About 3,000 people living at Dorking. Middle class well-off men and women of mixed ages, employed in the arts, professions, teaching etc. Quite a number have no need to work.	Social groups I, II and III. They are unconscious of their own spiritual needs. They are very much occupied with community and social work, and many think that being a Christian is a matter of doing good works.	1% Christian. Churches of all denominations are in the area, and there is evangelical outreach.	Mr John Le Boutillier 41 Hampstead Road Dorking Surrey RH4 3AE
S9	Over 750 people in a high density single road access council estate in Carshalton. There are many children and older people. Unemployment is common.	Social groups IV and V. Financial worries, relationship difficulties, depression and alcohol problems are primary concerns. There is apathy and a feeling that spiritual answers are not relevant to practical needs.	3% Christian. The Assemblies of God and the Sutton Christian Centre are in contact.	Mr and Mrs Mills 232 Durand Close Carshalton Surrey SM5 2BZ

OCCASIONAL GROUPS

O1	100 members of Surbiton Historical Society. Mostly elderly people who are or have been employed in management. Men and women. They meet monthly.	Social group II. They have no material needs. Their main concern is success in their business and social lives.	5% Christian. The Methodists and Anglicans have most contact.	Rev David Smith 24 Alexandra Drive Surbiton Surrey KT5 9AB

Description & Location	Characteristics	Openings for Outreach	Contact Person
O2 25 young women meeting in an afternoon club in Byfleet. They are aged 20-35 and work part-time or are housewives.	Social groups II and III. They are happy with their lives and feel no need for anything else.	10% Christian. Methodists in contact, but no outreach.	Mr Wallace White 9 Queen's Avenue Byfleet Weybridge Surrey KT14 7AD
O3 200 male and female employees of a Guildford insurance company. All grades of clerical and professional work and full age range of workers.	Social groups I, II and III. They are bound together by their work and need outreach and witness within that context.	3% Christian. There is outreach by Christian colleague. Churches with most contact are Anglican and Methodist.	n/a

Total population: 1,150,000

Estimated number
attending church: 86,000

**Total number not regularly
attending church: 1,064,000**

Non-attenders as
percentage of population: 93%

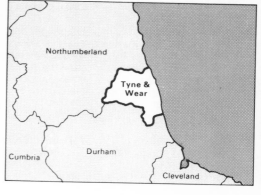

Number of people not regularly attending church:

Age		Sex	
Under 15:	223,000	**Men:**	511,000
15-19:	85,000	**Women:**	553,000
20-29:	160,000		
30-44:	192,000		
45-64:	255,000		
65 or over:	149,000		

SOCIAL/COMMUNITY GROUPS

	Description & Location	Characteristics	Openings for Outreach	Contact Person
S1	A large council estate in Sunderland with about 1,000 homes. Mixed ages and mainly employed in heavy engineering. Many unemployed.	Social groups III, IV and V. They consider that the Social Services meet all their needs. They do not want spiritual things.	Number of Christians negligible. Church of England, Roman Catholics, Free Baptists, Brethren and Nazarene all have contact. Nazarenes do door-to-door work.	Mr G M Goff 1 Fordenbridge Square Sunderland SR4 0BA
S2	A large number of people in Dunston, 95% of the population, who have very varied employment. Large numbers of old and young people.	All social classes. They do not feel the need of God, not even in times of distress.	The established churches have contact, especially through christenings, weddings and funerals.	Rev R J Teal The Methodist Manse 75 Mountside Gardens Dunston Gateshead NE11 9QD
S3	Students at the Polytechnic at Newcastle-upon-Tyne. They live in halls of residence and flats. Men and women, mainly between 19 and 22.	Non-manual whose main pre-occupations are alcohol and larger grants. They see people in the Church as hypocrites and they are ignorant of the Gospel.	1-2% Christian. There is a Campus Crusade for Christ and a Christian Fellowship. Also Church of England, URC and Baptist churches.	Mrs Ruth Maguire 90 Doncaster Road Sandyford Newcastle-upon-Tyne NE2 1RA
S4	People living on new estates in the suburbs of Newcastle on Tyne. Estates range in size from 500 to 3,000. Newly marrieds in private housing, employed in clerical work, local government or in the Civil Service. All 20-30 age group.	Non-manual social group. Concerned with financial security and better houses. Apathetic and sometimes hostile to the Christian message.	2% Christian. The parish church has contact with some of them.	n/a

TYNE & WEAR

	Description & Location	Characteristics	Openings for Outreach	Contact Person
E1	A group of about 40 Vietnamese Boat People settled at Wallsend by the Ockenden Venture. In local authority housing. All age groups and virtually all unemployed.	5% can read English easily. Their mother tongue is Vietnamese. Main problems are isolation, poverty and the culture gap.	A few Christians. They have had at least one English family befriending them.	n/a
E2	Many hundreds of immigrants mainly from Pakistan and surrounding areas living in Elswick area of Newcastle on Tyne. They work in local shops; many have been opened by them. There are many children.	25% read English easily. They have various languages and they are Hindu, Sikh and Muslim.	No known Christians. There has been some outreach.	n/a

Total population: 477,000

Estimated number
attending church: 47,000

**Total number not regularly
attending church: 430,000**

Non-attenders as
percentage of population: 90%

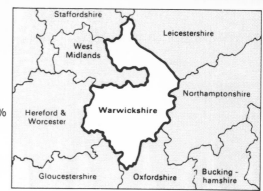

Number of people not regularly attending church:

Age		Sex	
Under 15:	99,000	**Men:**	211,000
15-19:	34,000	**Women:**	219,000
20-29:	60,000		
30-44:	86,000		
45-64:	99,000		
65 or over:	52,000		

SOCIAL/COMMUNITY GROUPS

	Description & Location	Characteristics	Openings for Outreach	Contact Person
S1	Dwellers on a mobile home park in 20 mobile homes in Nuneaton. Many retired.	Social class III and IV.	15% Christian. Anglican contact and regular visiting.	Mr Clive Buckler No 8 Res Castle View Castle Road Hartshill Nuneaton CV10 0SF
S2	A mining community of 3,000 in Nuneaton. About 17% unemployed; the rest work in mining or engineering.	Social class III, IV and V. They have a poor self-image. Conscious of poor prospects and boredom. Family ties are very important. Religion appears as a service done to them by outsiders — not anything they are personally committed to.	2% Christian. Anglican contact.	Rev T M Gouldstone The Vicarage Birmingham Road Ansley Nuneaton CV10 9PS
S3	2,000 young adults living on a new estate at Leamington Spa. Most are in their 20s or 30s and employed in local engineering factories.	Social class III. They are not conscious of any needs until trouble arises. Main concerns are working and paying the mortgage. No need of the Church.	1% Christian. Anglican and RC contact.	Rev A B Gardner Whitmarsh Rectory 2 Church Close Leamington Spa Warwicks CV31 2HJ
S4	A village within reach of Birmingham and Coventry. 500 affluent businessmen, solicitors, accountants etc, middle-aged with teenaged or adult children.	Social class I and II. They are people who have everything materially — 'the riches and worries of this life crowd out and choke them'.	10% Christian. Anglican contact, visitation.	n/a
S5	Young families living on a village-style estate at Warwick. About 700 men and women in mixed employment.	Social class III. Their concerns are personal identity and fulfilment. Their life is full of activity, with no need to refer to God.	3% Christian. Anglican, Brethren, RC, Methodist and Baptist contact.	Mr T Johnson The Vicarage Budbrooke Warwick CV35 8QL

Description & Location	Characteristics	Openings for Outreach	Contact Person
S6 A group of 1,000 affluent middle-class people living in Barford and employed as teachers, doctors, architects etc. Mostly middle-aged.	Social class I and II. Apathetic about church; they fear the financial or time commitment it may involve.	5% Christian. Anglican contact.	n/a

OCCASIONAL GROUPS

Description & Location	Characteristics	Openings for Outreach	Contact Person
O1 500 members of a squash club near Warwick. Men and women variously employed.	They are looking for personal fulfilment and satisfaction. For them life is complete, with no need for God.	2% Christian. Anglican, RC and Baptist contact.	Mr T Johnson The Vicarage Budbrooke Warwick CV35 8QL
O2 40 young married men and women who meet for social activities, outings etc. Employed in offices or small businesses.	Social class III. As they are happy, healthy and fairly well off, they need nothing materially and feel they have no need of the Gospel.	5% Christian. Anglican and Baptist contact.	n/a
O3 30 retired people in an Old People's Club at Nuneaton. Men and women, unskilled.	Social class V. They suffer from loneliness and are very set in their ways.	1% Christian. Regular visitation by Anglican minister.	n/a

Total population: 2,667,000

Estimated number
attending church: 203,000

**Total number not regularly
attending church: 2,464,000**

Non-attenders as
percentage of population: 92%

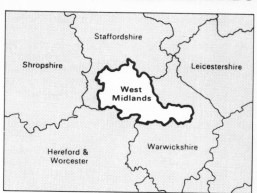

Number of people not regularly attending church:

Age		Sex	
Under 15:	542,000	**Men:**	1,207,000
15-19:	197,000	**Women:**	1,257,000
20-29:	345,000		
30-44:	468,000		
45-64:	592,000		
65 or over:	320,000		

SOCIAL/COMMUNITY GROUPS

	Description & Location	Characteristics	Openings for Outreach	Contact Person
S1	Market retailers and their labour force in Birmingham. About 450 employed on small-holdings and farms.	Social class III, IV and V. Very great pressure of working life, no time for religion except on holiday.	1% Christian. There is a Market Chaplain.	Mr Peter Hall 37 Barlows Road Birmingham B15 2PN
S2	Mixed community of 12,000 living in a residential area of Coventry, both council and private. Mixed age range. Mainly employed in banking, middle management, law and in factories.	Social class II and III. Their concerns are mainly material and they fail to see that God is relevant to their whole lives.	25% Christian. There is united outreach by all churches.	Rev R Woodward 23 The Chesics Styvechale Coventry CU2 5BD
S3	Inhabitants of tower blocks and maisonettes in the inner city of Birmingham. Very many unemployed, few stable homes and marriages. Men and women, all ages, West Indian and white. Unskilled.	Social class V. Main concerns are money and jobs. There is almost total ignorance about the Christian faith and the people are apathetic about it.	The number of Christians is not known. Anglican-run community shop and coffee bar. RC and Black churches contact.	n/a
S4	About 6,000 middle-class families living near Sutton Coldfield, mostly working in middle management.	Social class II. Dissatis-fied with their ambitions. They have little social contact, and there are many lonely wives. Their ambition and the time needed for work prevents them hearing the Gospel.	10% Christian. Anglican visitation.	Mr M J Smith 98 Kempson Ave Sutton Coldfield B72 1HQ
S5	1,600 residents of a council estate in Walsall. Factory workers and unemployed. Mixed ages.	Social class III, IV and V. Main concerns are more money and house repairs. They consider Jesus Christ is for the middle-class church.	Less than 1% Christian. Anglican services at the school and house groups. Also Methodist contact.	Rev David Butterfield 14 St Thomas Close Aldridge Walsall WS9 8SL

	Description & Location	Characteristics	Openings for Outreach	Contact Person
S6	20,000 living on council estates at Stourbridge. Factory workers and unemployed. Many young people.	Social class III, IV and V. There is worry over the break up of family life and financial problems. Apathetic towards the Church.	2% Christian. Free Church, Pentecostal and Anglican contact.	n/a
S7	About 4,000 working-class residents in Birmingham. Mostly middle-aged, factory workers, cleaners etc.	Social class III and IV. Conscious of financial material and social problems. The Church seems irrelevant taking time and money. Lack of knowledge about religion.	5% Christian. RC, Anglican and Baptist contact.	Pastor F C Williams 18 Rowley Grove Birmingham B33 0AS
S8	A group of all ages centred around the Sparkbrook Family Centre, mostly unemployed or manual workers. Many elderly.	Social class IV. They are conscious of the problems of the inner city and do not see the relevance of Christianity.	5% Christian. Anglican and Methodist contact.	n/a
S9	50,000 living at West Bromwich; traditional working-class Black Country people. Mostly they live in council houses. Most are manual workers in industry or in public services.	Social class III, IV and V. They are trying to preserve their traditional way of life in face of unemployment and immigration. They resent what they see as the comfortably-off Christians of the south.	5% Christian. Anglican, Methodist and Pentecostal contact; but not very effective.	n/a
S10	In Birmingham about 10,000 people a year who only attend St Peter's Church for baptisms, weddings and funerals. All types and all ages.	Social class III. They need to be taught about God's blessing and the power to love, and they need reassurance on resurrection. They have a fear of being trapped into regular church-going.	5% Christian. Outreach by the vicar and the congregation of St Peter's.	Rev Michael Counsell Harborne Vicarage Old Church Road Birmingham B17 0BB

ETHNIC/LINGUISTIC GROUPS

	Description & Location	Characteristics	Openings for Outreach	Contact Person
E1	Young people mainly from Hong Kong, mostly involved with the restaurant and retail trade in Birmingham.	Very few read English easily. Mother tongue is Cantonese; religion is Buddhism and Confucianism. Materialism and Chinese traditions keep them from the Gospel.	Few Christians. There is a church service and visitation and a school caters for the children.	Mr Jerry Eng 734 Bristol Road Selly Oak Birmingham B29 6DH
E2	About 400 from India living in West Bromwich. Factory or clerical workers.	About 60% can read English. Mother tongue is Punjabi; religion is Sikh.	2% Christian. Anglican contact.	Rev J Trevor Glover Holy Trinity Vicarage Burlington Road West Bromwich B70 6LF

	Description & Location	Characteristics	Openings for Outreach	Contact Person
E3	In the Lozells area of Birmingham. 5,000 from Pakistan and Bangladesh, working in restaurants, shops, factories. Many children.	60% read English. Mother tongues are Urdu and Bengali; religion is Islam. There is a rigid adherence to the Muslim culture and creed enforced by religious and social leaders. There is a need for employment for the young.	No known Christians. Two Christian groups have services in Urdu. Personal witness, counselling, a bookshop and Advice Centre for family problems.	Rev D H Dansey 92 Lozells Road Lozells Birmingham B19 2TB
E4	Thousands of young people of Caribbean origin around Birmingham: second-generation immigrants. Many unemployed; others are in clerical, manual or nursing jobs.	90% read English. Mother tongue is English; they are nominal Christians. Apathetic towards the Church, seen as white-dominated.	Some parents try to influence their children.	Rev G Lee 14 Howard Road Yardley Birmingham B25 8AL
E5	4,000 immigrants from India and Pakistan at Lye, Stourbridge. Many are unemployed but a large number are shopkeepers.	50% read English. Mother tongues are Urdu and Punjabi; religion is Islam. They consider Christianity a white man's religion.	No regular outreach. The church services are in English.	Mr S R Buck 37 Worcester Street Stourbridge DY8 1AT
E6	Asian immigrants in Wolverhampton, 34% of population. High unemployment; others work in shops and industry. Many young people.	50% read English. Mother tongues are Hindi, Urdu and Punjabi; religion is Sikh. They cling to conservative, nationalistic and religious things to preserve their identity.	2% Christian. There is an Asian Christian Fellowship.	Rev E Malcolm St Luke's Vicarage 122 Goldthorn Hill Wolverhampton WV2 3MU
E7	Many thousands of Asian families living around Bearwood, Smethwick and one side of Edgbaston. They are from India and Pakistan. Factory and office workers; many unemployed. Many young people.	60% can read English. Mother tongue is Urdu or Punjabi; religion is Hindu or Islam. They reject Christ.	1% are Christian. There is a church with a community centre and an Asian community worker plus a children's mission.	Mr Andrew Nix 73 Laxley Road Edgbaston Birmingham B16 0JQ
E8	About 500 Pakistanis in Birmingham. Mostly shopkeepers or unemployed. Many young children.	Only the children read English easily. Mother tongue is Punjabi; religion is Sunni Muslim. They have a fixed Muslim social background.	No Christians. Only normal parish outreach which touches them little.	n/a

Description & Location	Characteristics	Openings for Outreach	Contact Person
E9 About 4,000 in a Jewish community scattered around Edgbaston, Moseley and Solihull.	95% read English. Mother tongue is English but some have other European languages as well. Their religion is Judaism. Concerned about anti-semitism.	There are about 30 Christians. There is the CMJ and the West Midlands Messianic Fellowship.	CMJ Headquarters 10 Clarence Road St Albans Herts AL1 4NE
E10 West Indian immigrants in Wolverhampton, approx 15% of population. High unemployment; others work in transport and industry. Many young people.	Most read English. Mother tongue is English, religions are Rasta and nominal Christianity. Young people often alienated from family.	60% nominally Christian. Many groups have contact.	Rev E Malcolm St Luke's Vicarage 122 Goldthorn Hill Wolverhampton WV2 3MU

OCCASIONAL GROUPS

Description & Location	Characteristics	Openings for Outreach	Contact Person
O1 About 30 young glue-sniffers in West Bromwich, mostly unemployed.	Social class IV and V. Need caring counselling facilities.	No known Christians. Pentecostal church contact.	Mr C B Gardner 58 Esher Road West Bromwich B71 1QR
O2 Many long-term unemployed in Birmingham; young people living in various hostels. 30 attend the Central Hall. Mostly men.	Social class IV and V. Searching for self-esteem and fulfilment, they are suspicious of Christians and view them as hypocrites. But they are open to caring service by Christians.	No known Christians. Methodist, Salvation Army, Anglican and Baptist contact.	Mr W G Krouwell Birmingham Central Hall Corporation Street Birmingham B4 6QW
O3 A group of 250 who attend Working Men's Clubs in Wakefield. All are council tenants, employed in mines or labouring.	Social class IV and V. Their main concerns are broken families, emotional instability and financial worries. The desire to appear masculine and pressure from the group keep them from the Gospel.	No known Christians. No known outreach.	Rev Alan Bain 39 Frome Road Odd Down Bath Avon BA2 2QF

Total population: 673,000

Estimated number attending church: 54,000

Total number not regularly attending church: 619,000

Non-attenders as percentage of population: 92%

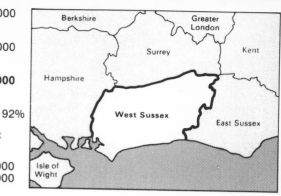

Number of people not regularly attending church:

Age		Sex	
Under 15:	111,000	**Men:**	297,000
15-19:	43,000	**Women:**	322,000
20-29:	87,000		
30-44:	105,000		
45-64:	149,000		
65 or over:	124,000		

SOCIAL/COMMUNITY GROUPS

	Description & Location	Characteristics	Openings for Outreach	Contact Person
S1	60 retired men and women in sheltered housing for the elderly, with a warden, on a council estate.	Unskilled social group. There is a need for companionship and practical help.	20% Christian. The Evangelical church is in contact and there is outreach through women's meeting, hymn singing etc.	n/a
S2	40% of the population of Worthing, living on bungalow estates. All old and retired people.	Non-manual group III. Conscious of loneliness, boredom and aimlessness. Disillusioned and world weary attitude, combined with rigidity of thinking, keeps them from the Gospel.	10% Christian. There is Anglican contact.	n/a
S3	Several thousands of people living at Crawley. Principally middle-aged, many working on service duties at Gatwick airport.	Social groups IV and V. Concerned with material well-being and acquisition of luxury items. No awareness of the relevance of the Gospel.	The number of Christians is very small. There are chaplains at the airport and churches in the area.	Rev A F Hawker St Mary's Rectory Forester Road Southgate Crawley West Sussex RH10 6EH
S4	160 residents on two council estates at Ardingly. Full age range. Working manually for the council or in local factories. Men and women.	Social group IV. Money appears to be their main concern. There is a lack of effective meeting ground with Christians.	2% Christians. There is personal contact from the parish church.	Rev David Perryman The Rectory Church Lane Ardingly Haywards Heath West Sussex RH17 6UR
S5	Over 8,000 people on a council estate north of Littlehampton. Most work is in local factories. Normal age range.	Social groups IV and V. The church is seen as middle class. There seems to be a lack of commitment on the part of some of the local churches.	1% Christian. There are two Free Evangelical churches, as well as Baptist and Anglican churches. A little outreach attempted.	Mr Robin Gammon 2a Connaught Road Littlehampton West Sussex BN17 6ER

WEST SUSSEX

ETHNIC/LINGUISTIC GROUPS

	Description & Location	Characteristics	Openings for Outreach	Contact Person
E1	2,000 Asians in the neighbourhood of Crawley, from Pakistan or India. Employed in manual work at Gatwick or on an industrial estate. Normal age range.	Their mother tongue is Urdu, and their religion is Islam. There is a language barrier and a ghetto mentality.	No known Christians or outreach.	Rev I Prior Broadfield Vicarage 10 Colonsay Road Broadfield Crawley West Sussex RH11 9DF

Total population:	2,063,000
Estimated number attending church:	152,000
Total number not regularly attending church:	**1,911,000**
Non-attenders as percentage of population:	93%

Number of people not regularly attending church:

Age		Sex	
Under 15:	420,000	**Men:**	917,000
15-19:	153,000	**Women:**	994,000
20-29:	268,000		
30-44:	344,000		
45-64:	439,000		
65 or over:	287,000		

SOCIAL/COMMUNITY GROUPS

	Description & Location	Characteristics	Openings for Outreach	Contact Person
S1	A group of one-parent families and members of broken homes in North Halifax, mainly in their 20s and 30s. High unemployment.	Social class IV and V. They have a fear of authority and a sense of failure; they want to belong. They look on Church as remote, unreal and middle class.	1% Christian. Anglican and Elim contact.	Rev C P Edmondson St George's Vicarage Lee Mount Halifax HX3 5BT
S2	20,000 living in the inner-city area of Leeds. Men and women of all ages, unemployed miners, labourers etc.	Social class IV and V. Low achievers, requiring better social conditions. They are antagonistic to the Gospel and have a persecution complex.	1% Christian. There are local house groups and there are churches in the area.	n/a
S3	About 30,000 living on large council estates around Huddersfield. All ages. Most are employed on assembly lines in textiles or light industry.	Social class III, IV and V. Very conscious of the need for job security, more money, and leisure activities. They see the Church as irrelevant and are unaware of any spiritual need.	1% Christian. Some churches have a strong programme of witness.	n/a
S4	About 200 retired people living around Liversedge, in special accommodation, flats and bungalows. The majority are women who were employed in the carpet industry etc.	Social class III and IV. Fear of loneliness, incapacity and death. They have not associated with the Christian churches for years.	10% Christian. Services are held for residents and there is a club for the disabled. The nearest church is Methodist.	Rev Eileen Wright 10 Knowler Hill Liversedge West Yorkshire WF15 6PH
S5	A group on a council estate near Drighlington; several problem families. Many children and young people. Unskilled labouring.	Social class IV and V. Their main concerns are financial and material; they do not see the relevance of the Gospel to their needs.	1% Christian. There are churches in the area.	n/a

	Description & Location	Characteristics	Openings for Outreach	Contact Person
S6	50 old people living in a community near Pudsey, all retired.	Social class III. Great need for caring. Indifference to the Gospel.	20% Christian. Anglican and Methodist contact.	Rev B K Asare 2 Mount Pleasant Road Pudsey West Yorkshire LS28 7DY
S7	Groups of 20-30 teenagers (13 to 15 years) in Baildon. Still at school.	Their lives are aimless; their needs are those of the whole community. There is ignorance of the Gospel and the general materialistic and physical attitude of our time.	Very few Christians. Methodist and RC contact. There is a centre where they are welcome.	Mr Ian Lewis 8 Cecil Avenue Baildon Shipley BD17 5LN
S8	About 600 working-class families living on council estates at Methley. Mixed age range.	Social class III, IV and V. The main concerns are employment and boredom. There is a feeling that the Church belongs to an alien culture, that the local church has been unwelcoming and dull. Church people in the past have not tried to overcome barriers.	4 or 5 Christians. Anglican contact.	Rev M Whittock The Rectory Methley Leeds LS26 9BJ
S9	A group of 800-1,000 teenagers and young people, some married. They come together on street corners and in pubs at Methley.	All social classes. Mainly conscious of boredom and unemployment. They consider the Church is old and lifeless; they have no time for spiritual things.	1% Christian. Anglican, Methodist and Pentecostal contact.	Rev M Whittock The Rectory Methley Leeds LS26 9BJ
S10	800 living in poor quality housing on an estate in Halifax. Almost 100% unemployment; many children.	Social class V. Worry about finance, drink and violence. The culture of Christianity and worship far removed from their problems.	No known Christians. RC contact.	Rev Gordon Dem Jumpeter Parsonage Mixenden Halifax HX2 8RX

ETHNIC/LINGUISTIC GROUPS

	Description & Location	Characteristics	Openings for Outreach	Contact Person
E1	10,000 from Pakistan, living in Bradford, unskilled and mainly unemployed.	10% read English easily. Mother tongue is Urdu; religion is Islam.	No known outreach.	n/a
E2	Several thousand Asian immigrants from Pakistan or Kenya, living in a run down area of Halifax.	Most of the men read English and some of the women. Mother tongue is Urdu; religion is Islam.	Very few Christians. The local vicar concentrates on friendly contacts.	n/a

Description & Location	Characteristics	Openings for Outreach	Contact Person
E3 Thousands in Bradford inner city, from Asia, Eastern Europe and West Indies. All ages from a variety of countries. Most are now unemployed.	Many languages; religions include Hindu, Muslim, Sikh and Orthodox. Their common problems are unemployment, poor housing and racial prejudice.	'Outreach of Bradford' is working among them.	n/a

OCCASIONAL GROUPS

O1 80 people meeting on church premises; special interest in sport. Young people with varied employment.	All social classes. No spiritual awareness, only material.	10% Christian. Methodist contact.	Rev B K Asare 2 Mount Pleasant Road Pudsey West Yorkshire LS28 7DY

WILTSHIRE

Total population:	528,000
Estimated number attending church:	50,000
Total number not regularly attending church:	**478,000**
Non-attenders as percentage of population:	91%

Number of people not regularly attending church:

Age		Sex	
Under 15:	110,000	**Men:**	239,000
15-19:	43,000	**Women:**	239,000
20-29:	77,000		
30-44:	91,000		
45-64:	100,000		
65 or over:	57,000		

SOCIAL/COMMUNITY GROUPS

	Description & Location	Characteristics	Openings for Outreach	Contact Person
S1	About 500 living on 2 new estates at Trowbridge. Mostly young families in mixed employment.	Social class I, II and III. Not conscious of any needs.	5% Christian. Anglican and Baptist contact.	n/a
S2	Older and well established country folk in the vale of Pewsey. Engaged in farming.	Social class III, IV and V. They feel that outsiders have taken over their area. They have a confused folk-religion.	10% Christian. Anglican contact.	n/a
S3	People living in country areas near Salisbury with varied occupations. Mixed ages.	Social class III and IV. Not interested in the Gospel. Attend church only for baptisms, weddings, funerals.	1% Christian. Anglican contact.	Rev R Sharpe Redlynch Vicarage Nr Salisbury Wiltshire SP5 2PE
S4	About 100 council house tenants in a village near Swindon. Mixed employment.	Social class III. Concerned with material security. Feel that the Church is only for weddings, funerals etc.	5% Christian. Anglican contact.	n/a
S5	5,000 living in Swindon. Most work for British Rail.	Social class III and IV. Strong sense of community. They see the Church as irrelevant.	4% Christian. Visitation and Baptist, Anglican and Salvation Army contact.	Mr David Howell 72 Malvern Road Gorse Hill Swindon SN2 1AU

OCCASIONAL GROUPS

O1	About 100 members of a sports club at Burbage. Young to middle aged. Mostly employed in clerical work.	Social class III. Main concern is their children's schooling. They are very materialistic and not conscious of the need for salvation.	2% Christian. Anglican contact.	Mr Jeremy Anderson The Vicarage East Court Burbage Wiltshire SN8 3AG

Description & Location	Characteristics	Openings for Outreach	Contact Person
O2 A group of 150 young mothers and sometimes fathers who meet their children and attend PTA and other school activities at Warminster.	Social class I, II and III. Not conscious of any great needs. Worries are about children. Many are well disposed to the Church but not prepared to play an active part.	4% Christian. Anglican contact.	Rev Fred Woods Christ Church Vicarage Avon Road Warminster BA12 9PR
O3 About 35 members of various sports clubs at Broadchalke. Young people working in farms and offices.	Social class III and IV. Concerned with their own needs and pleasures. No concept of Christian discipline in their lives.	Number of Christians not known. Anglican contact.	Mrs M Tryhorn 6 Knighton Road Broadchalke Salisbury Wiltshire SP5 5DX

WALES

Total population:	2,809,000
Estimated number attending church:	406,000
Total number not regularly attending church:	**2,403,000**
Non-attenders as percentage of population:	86%

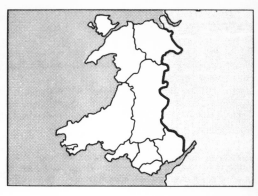

Number of people not regularly attending church:

Age		Sex	
Under 15:	481,000	**Men:**	1,201,000
15-19:	192,000	**Women:**	1,202,000
20-29:	384,000		
30-44:	433,000		
45-64:	577,000		
65 or over:	336,000		

SOCIAL/COMMUNITY GROUPS

Description & Location	Characteristics	Openings for Outreach	Contact Person
Clwyd			
S1 4,000 men and women of all ages living in Buckley. They work in a variety of jobs.	All social groups, but mainly skilled-manual and semi-skilled. Many would attend church for special services. They lack a 'living' Faith.	90% nominal Christians. All the mainstream denominations have churches. Visitation, Pram and Toddler services and Youth groups are a means of outreach.	Rev Edward Price St Matthew's Vicarage Church Road Buckley Clwyd CH7 3JN
S2 35 men and women in Corrig-y-Drudion. All involved in farming. Mixed age range.	Social classes III, IV and V. Material needs are a major concern.	The Church in Wales has the most contact with the group. There are also three chapels.	n/a
S3 The inhabitants of a large council estate at Wrexham. Some of the housing is of poor quality. There are many young marrieds. Unemployment is high. Many work on the shop floor of factories.	Social classes IV and V. Financial needs are most important. Religion appears irrelevant and the Church is often seen as an oppressive force.	Number of Christians not known. The Roman Catholic Church has the most contact. There are also other churches in the area.	Mr Stephen Heap 43 Price's Lane Rhosddu Wrexham Clwyd LL11 2WB
Dyfed			
S4 Some 2,000 students at the University of Wales, Aberystwyth. Most live on the campus; others live in the town.	Concerned with finance and career prospects. Most are satisfied with their life style.	10% Christian. The Christian Union is active. The Evangelical congregations of the Anglican, URC, Elim, Baptist and Methodist Churches have most contact.	n/a

Description & Location	Characteristics	Openings for Outreach	Contact Person
Gwynedd			
S5 4,000 living on a large council estate at Holyhead. The main employment is with British Rail and Anglesey Aluminium. Many are unemployed. There are many young folk and a number of elderly people too.	Semi-skilled social class. Their main concerns are employment and finance. Unemployment, materialism, apathy and a Church seen as middle-class cuts them off from the Gospel.	2% Christian. The Anglican, Roman Catholic and Presbyterian churches have contact. Individual Christian witness to the others and Mission to Youth are the main forms of outreach.	n/a
Mid Glamorgan			
S6 2,000 people living on two council estates in Cwmbach near Aberdare. Most would have only occasional jobs.	Social class IV. Security of employment is a real need. Family ties are strong. The Church is seen as too respectable.	1% Christian. The Church in Wales and the Pentecostal church are in contact. There is also a Nonconformist Welsh-speaking chapel in the area.	n/a
S7 A group of elderly folk, mainly retired miners and their wives, in Hengoed and Ystrad Mynach.	Mostly social group IV. They feel a need for social fellowship. Their reasons for being cut off from the Gospel are varied and individual.	A few Christians. Weekly meetings are held. The Independent Baptist Mission has contact with the group.	n/a
S8 500 young families on a new estate at Rhydyfelin, most of whom work on construction sites or in shops, but a large percentage are unemployed.	Social classes IV and V. They do not consider that the Church has any relevance to their lives. Due to ignorance many have a fear of being committed to the Church.	No known Christians. The nearest church is about 1/2 mile away. Note that the Jehovah's Witnesses are active.	n/a
West Glamorgan			
S9 Some 2,000 men and women of all ages living on a post-war housing estate, mainly council owned, in Craigfellen, Clydach.	Semi-skilled workers. The group would be conscious of their social needs. They appear indifferent to the Gospel.	10% Christian. The Baptist Church is most active among this group. The Church in Wales and the Roman Catholic Church are also present.	n/a

ETHNIC/LINGUISTIC GROUPS

Description & Location	Characteristics	Openings for Outreach	Contact Person
Clwyd			
E1 A small Chinese community in Wrexham employed mainly in the catering trade. They live mostly in the town centre. There are many young people in the group.	Speaking English proves more difficult than reading it. They are conscious of their need to learn English and Welsh. Their language problems cut them off from the Gospel.	There are some Christians in the group. The City Temple carries out visitation.	Mr Stephen Heap 43 Price's Lane Wrexham Clwyd LL11 2WB

South Glamorgan

Description & Location	Characteristics	Openings for Outreach	Contact Person
E2 Several thousand folk of Chinese extraction living in Cardiff. They live in the Riverside area of the city and have been in Cardiff for some 10-15 years. Most work in the catering trade.	90% would read English easily. They feel a need for security. Affluence tends to cut them off from the Gospel.	No known Christian outreach.	n/a
E3 Many folk of Jamaican origin living in the Docks area of Cardiff. A wide age range. Many used to work with the ships. There are various types of employment now.	Their background is originally Christian. Now there is little desire to participate in the Good News.	5% Christian. There is a mission in the Docks and several other churches.	Rev Alex Tee 39 Cowbridge Road East The City Temple Cardiff CF1 9AD
E4 Several thousand Pakistani people living in down-town Cardiff. A wide age range.	Their religions are various. Some 75% would read English easily. Language tends to be a barrier to the Gospel. A lack of Christian literature is also a handicap.	It is uncertain whether there are any Christians in the group. The City Temple is involved in outreach through a youth club.	Rev Alex Tee 39 Cowbridge Road East The City Temple Cardiff CF1 9AD
E5 A group of 20 mothers who meet at a Welsh language playgroup.	The possibility of meeting to speak in Welsh and ensure that their children hear and speak Welsh is important.	There is a Welsh Chapel. The number of Christians in the group is not known. Welsh Sunday Schools and Church involvement in their activities would provide a means of outreach.	Mrs C Pavelin 33 Barberry Rise Penarth S Glamorgan CF6 1RB

OCCASIONAL GROUPS

Clwyd

Description & Location	Characteristics	Openings for Outreach	Contact Person
O1 A group of some 60 women in a Mothers and Toddlers group in Rhos on Sea. Most have moved into the area because of their husbands' work. They meet once a week.	Social classes I, II and III. They are often lonely and have a great need for friendship in what is a strange and new environment. The Church is seen as irrelevant to their needs. Apathy and materialism cuts them off from the Gospel.	10% Christian. The Church in Wales and the Methodist church have contact. The Mothers' Union and the Anglican church are attempting to reach the group.	Rev R Roberts Llandrillo Vicarage Colwyn Bay Clwyd LL28 4UD

Dyfed

Description & Location	Characteristics	Openings for Outreach	Contact Person
O2 A group of 12 women in Pembroke whose aim is to benefit those in need locally. They are in association with the Round Table. They meet monthly.	Social groups I and II. They are conscious of medical needs and poverty not being met by other agencies. They lead busy lives and do not realise the importance of the Gospel.	1 Christian. The Church of England and the Baptist church are in contact. Personal evangelism is needed.	Pastor R James 70 Main Street Pembroke Dyfed SA71 4HH

Description & Location	Characteristics	Openings for Outreach	Contact Person
South Glamorgan			
O3 Several hundred folk in Cardiff who spend much of their time in Bingo Halls and Community Centres. Many are senior citizens; the others are in varied employment.	Social classes IV and V. They would see their main need as one of social contact. They have little desire for the Gospel.	2% Christian. There are many churches in the area. The City Temple carries out visitation in some of the Community Centres.	Rev Alex Tee 39 Cowbridge Road East The City Temple Cardiff CF1 9AD
O4 20 to 30 members of a Badminton group meeting twice weekly in Penarth. They work as housewives or are employed as teachers and accountants.	Social classes I and III. The group meets out of a need to fill time, keep fit and socialise. Many are complacent and comfortable with their lives.	20% Christian. The Baptist church has the most contact. There is informal witnessing to the group. Church-based keep-fit clubs and women's groups would be a means of outreach.	Mrs G Cook 2 Fennel Close Penarth South Glamorgan CF6 1QF
West Glamorgan			
O5 A young wives' group with 40 members in a new private housing area in Swansea. They meet weekly. They are employed mainly as secretaries or teachers.	Social groups I, II and III. Their main concerns are the education of their children and their social status. Complacency and agnosticism keep them from the Gospel.	45% Christian. The Anglican church has contact. Visiting Christian speakers provide an opportunity for outreach.	Chancellor M Hughes The Vicarage 30 Goetre Fach Rd Killay Swansea SA2 7SG

SUBJECT INDEX

Affluent
Avon S4
Buckinghamshire S2
Cheshire S1, S3, O5
Essex S4, S6
Greater London S1, S9
Hertfordshire S3, S9
Kent S6
Lancashire S9
Leicestershire S1, S8
Norfolk S4
Somerset S1, S3
Surrey S3, S8
Warwickshire S4, S6

Arabic
Greater London E5

Armed Forces
Cornwall S6, S7
Hampshire S5, S8
Suffolk S5

Bangladesh
Lancashire E1
West Midlands E3

Bed-sits
Dorset S2
Greater London O2, O7
Hampshire O2
Merseyside S1
Surrey S5

Bengali
Hertfordshire E1
West Midlands E3

British Legion
Suffolk O3

Buddhists
Greater Manchester E4
Kent E3
Nottinghamshire E1
West Midlands E1

Cantonese
Greater Manchester E4
West Midlands E1
Wales E2

Chinese
Suffolk E1
Wales E1, E2

Community Centre
Merseyside O4

Commuters
Essex S11
Greater London S1, S9, O5

Hertfordshire S5, S9, S10
Kent S7, S11
Leicestershire S2
Oxford S1

Confucians
West Midlands E1

Council Estates
Avon S2, S3
Bedfordshire S1
Cambridgeshire S2
Cheshire S4
Cleveland S1
Cornwall S1
Cumbria S3
Derbyshire S3, S5
Devon S1
East Sussex S1, S3
Essex S5, S6, S8, S9, S13
Greater London S3, S4, S7
Greater Manchester S1, S2, S8
Hampshire S4, S6, S8
Herefordshire S1, S2
Hertfordshire S6, S7
Humberside S1
Kent S3, S9, S11, S12
Lancashire S3, S5, S6, S7, S8,
  S12, S13
Leicestershire S4
Lincolnshire S1
Norfolk S1, S3, S6, S8, S11
North Yorkshire S2, S4
Northamptonshire S1
Northumberland S2
Oxfordshire S2, S3
Shropshire S1, S2
South Yorkshire S1, S6
Staffordshire S3, S4, S5
Surrey S1
West Midlands S3, S5, S6
West Sussex S4
West Yorkshire S5, S8
Wales S3, S5, S6, S9

Drugs
East Sussex O1
Hampshire S9
Norfolk O2
West Midlands O1
West Sussex O1

East Africa
Greater Manchester E2
Kent E2

Elderly Clubs
Avon O5
Cheshire O1
Cornwall O1

Devon O1, O2, O3, O4
Kent O10
Leicestershire O1
North Yorkshire O4
Norfolk O3
South Yorkshire O1
Warwickshire O3

Elderly and Retired
Avon S5
Cornwall S3, S8
Durham S1
Essex S11, S15
Greater London S7
Greater Manchester S3
Hampshire O2
Merseyside S3
Norfolk S4, S5, S8
North Yorkshire S3
Northamptonshire S3
Northumberland S2
Nottinghamshire S5
Somerset S1, S3
Surrey S6
West Sussex S1, S2
West Yorkshire S4, S6
Wales S7

Factory Groups
Avon S1
Cambridgeshire S2, S4
Cornwall S2, S5
Derbyshire S1, S2, S6, S8
Essex S2, S10
Greater London S6
Humberside S4
Kent S2, S11
Lancashire S13
Norfolk S8, S11
Nottinghamshire S1
Oxfordshire S3, S4
Shropshire S1
Staffordshire S2
Warwickshire S3
West Sussex S4, S5
West Yorkshire S3

Gujerati
Derbyshire E1
Greater London E8, E11
Greater Manchester E1, E2, E6
Lancashire E1

Hebrew
Essex E1

Hindi
Greater London E7, E9, E13
Hertfordshire E1
West Midlands E6

Hindus
Berkshire E1
Derbyshire E1
Essex E1
Greater London E10
Greater Manchester E2, E6
Hampshire E2
Hertfordshire E1
Kent E3
Tyne and Wear E2
West Midlands E7
West Yorkshire E2

Holiday Makers
Dorset O2
Suffolk O1

Hong Kong
West Midlands E1

Illocano
North Yorkshire E1

India
Derbyshire E1
Greater London E10, E13
Greater Manchester E6
Kent E2
West Midlands E2, E5, E7

Islam
Greater London E5
Greater Manchester E1, E2
Hertfordshire E2
Lancashire E1
Norfolk E1
South Yorkshire E2

Jamaican
Cambridgeshire E1
Gloucestershire E1
Greater London E2, E6
Greater Manchester E5
West Midlands E10
Wales E3

Jews
Cheshire E1
Essex E1
Greater London E3, E12
Greater Manchester E3
Hertfordshire E3
West Midlands E9

Muslims
Berkshire E1
Cheshire E2
Derbyshire E1
Essex E1
Greater London E10, E11, E13
Greater Manchester E6
Hertfordshire E1
Kent E3
Lancashire E2
Norfolk E1
South Yorkshire E2, E3

Staffordshire E1
Tyne and Wear E2
West Midlands E5, E7
West Sussex E1
West Yorkshire E1, E2

Medical
Cheshire O2, O5
Devon O8
Kent O7, O9
Norfolk O4

Mobile Homes
Cumbria S4
Essex S3
Norfolk S2
Warwickshire S1

Mothers and Toddlers
Cambridgeshire O3
Cheshire O3
Cumbria O2
Derbyshire O2
Essex O1
Greater London O1, O11
Kent O8, O12
Lancashire O4
Lincolnshire O1
Norfolk O1
Northamptonshire O2
North Yorkshire S7
Nottinghamshire O4
Somerset O1
South Yorkshire O3
Wiltshire O2
Wales O1

Occupational
Avon S1
Berkshire S1
Buckinghamshire O3, O4
Cheshire S5
Devon S3
Durham S2
Hampshire S7
Hertfordshire S4
Kent S1, S3
Lancashire O1, O2, O5
North Yorkshire O3
Northamptonshire S5
Northumberland S1
Nottinghamshire S2, S3, O2
South Yorkshire S2, S8
Suffolk O1
Surrey O3
Warwickshire S2
West Midlands S1
West Sussex S3
Wiltshire S5

Pakistanis
Derbyshire E1
Gloucestershire E1
Greater Manchester E1, E6
Hertfordshire E2
Kent E2

Lancashire E2
South Yorkshire E2, E3
Staffordshire E1
West Midlands E3, E5, E7, E8
West Sussex E1
West Yorkshire E1
Wales E4

Private Estates
Avon S4
Bedfordshire S2
Cambridgeshire S1
Cornwall S4, S6
Derbyshire S4
Dorset S5
East Sussex S1
Essex S1, S4, S14
Greater Manchester S4
Hertfordshire S8
Kent S5, S10
Lancashire S4, S11, S14
North Yorkshire S5
Nottinghamshire S1, S6
South Yorkshire S5
Suffolk S5
Surrey S3
Tyne and Wear S4

Professional Groups
Avon S4
Cambridgeshire S7
Derbyshire S4
Dorset S3, S4
Greater London S2, S9, S12
Humberside S2
Kent S4, S5
Lancashire S11
Leicestershire S1, S2, S8
Northamptonshire S4
Oxfordshire S1, S5, S6
Surrey S7
Warwickshire S4, S6
West Midlands S2, S4

Punjabi
Berkshire E1
Derbyshire E1
Greater London E1, E13
Kent E1, E2
South Yorkshire E2
West Midlands E5, E6, E7, E8

Recreation
Avon O2
Hertfordshire O1
Merseyside O2, O3
North Yorkshire O1, O5
Surrey O1

Retired
See under Elderly

Romany
Buckinghamshire E1

Rotarians
Essex O5

Rural Groups
Berkshire S2
Buckinghamshire S1
Cambridgeshire S5
Cheshire S1
Derbyshire O1
Devon S2, S6
Hampshire S2, S3
Herefordshire S3
Lancashire S1
Leicestershire S2, S8
Norfolk S5, S7, S9, S13
North Yorkshire S1, S2
Northamptonshire S4
South Yorkshire S1
Suffolk S4
Warwickshire S1
Wiltshire S2, S3
Wales S2

Sikhs
Berkshire E1
Derbyshire E1
Essex E1
Greater London E1, E10
Hampshire E2
Kent E1, E2
Tyne and Wear E2
West Midlands E2, E6
West Yorkshire E3

Social Action
Bedford O2
Cheshire O5
Devon O3, O8
Essex O2
Greater Manchester O2
North Yorkshire O6
Somerset O2
Wales O2

Social Clubs
Berkshire O1
Cambridgeshire O1, O2
Cumbria O1
Essex O6
Warwickshire O2

Sports Groups
Berkshire O2
Devon O5
Essex O3, O4, O6
Greater London O14
Kent O1, O11
Merseyside O4
Nottinghamshire O3
Warwickshire O1
West Yorkshire O1
Wiltshire O1, O3
Wales O4

Students
Cambridgeshire S7
Greater London S10, O8, O12
Kent S5, O13
Leicestershire S5, S6
Norfolk S10
Oxfordshire S7
Tyne and Wear S3
West Yorkshire S7
Wales S4

Teenage Groups
Dorset O1
Greater London S10, O3, O4,
O9
Kent O13
Lancashire O3
Merseyside O1
Northamptonshire O1
Oxfordshire O2

Ugandan
Cheshire E2
Gloucestershire E1

Unemployed
Cheshire S7
Cleveland S3, S4
Dorset S1, S2
Durham S3
Greater London S8, S11, S16,
O6
Greater Manchester S2, S3
Lancashire S13
Nottinghamshire S1, S3
Shropshire S2
South Yorkshire S4, S5
Staffordshire S1, S3, S5
Surrey S9
Tyne and Wear S1
West Midlands S3, S5, S8
West Yorkshire S5, S10, E3
Wales S5, S8

Urdu
Derbyshire E1
Greater Manchester E2, E6
Hertfordshire E1
Lancashire E1, E2
South Yorkshire E1, E2, E3
West Midlands E3, E5
West Sussex E1
West Yorkshire E1, E2

Vagrants
Avon O3
Greater London S8, O10
Greater Manchester O1
West Midlands O2

Vietnamese
Greater London E4
Greater Manchester E4
Nottinghamshire E1
Suffolk E1
Tyne and Wear E1

Women's Institute
Cambridgeshire O4
Kent O3

Working Men's Clubs
Durham O1, O2
North Yorkshire O2
West Midlands O2

Youth Clubs
Avon O4
Buckinghamshire O2
Greater London O3, O4
Nottinghamshire O1
South Yorkshire O2
Staffordshire O1
Suffolk O2

LOCATION INDEX

148

Kendal, Cumbria S1, S2
Kidbrooke, Greater London E4
Kidsgrove, Staffordshire S5
Kimbolton, Cambridgeshire S5
King's Lynn, Norfolk S8
Kirkby, Cumbria O1
Kirkby in Ashfield,
    Nottinghamshire O4
Knebworth, Hertfordshire S3

Laleham, Greater London S2
Lancaster, Lancashire S9
Leamington Spa, Warwickshire
    S3
Leeds, West Yorkshire S2, S8,
    S9
Leicester, Leicestershire S6, S7
Leigh, Greater Manchester S5
Leigh, Kent S8
Leighton Buzzard, Bedfordshire
    S1, O1
Lichfield, Staffordshire S1
Lincoln, Lincolnshire S1
Liphook, Hampshire S8, E1
Littlehampton, West Sussex S5
Liverpool, Merseyside O2, O3,
    O4
Liversedge, West Yorkshire S4
Locking, Avon O1, O6
Longton, Staffordshire E1
Lowestoft, Suffolk O1
Lutterworth, Leicestershire S8
Lynn, Cheshire S6

Macclesfield, Cheshire S2
Madley, Herefordshire S2
Manchester, Greater Manchester
    S9, E3, E4, E5, O1
Market Drayton, Shropshire S1
Mayfield, East Sussex S2
Mayfield, Staffordshire S4
Middleton, Lancashire S13
Middleton, Norfolk O1
Milton Keynes, Buckinghamshire
    E1
Muswell Hill, Greater London O13

New Barnet, Hertfordshire S7
Newbury, Berkshire O2
Newham, Greater London O9
Newquay, Cornwall O1
Newcastle-upon-Tyne, Tyne and
    Wear S3, S4
Newton Flotman, Norfolk S13
Northallerton, North Yorkshire
    S2, S5
Norwich, Norfolk S2, S10, E1,
    O2
Northampton, Northamptonshire
    S1, S2
Nottingham, Nottinghamshire S1,
    S3, S4, S5, E1, O2
Nuneaton, Warwickshire S1,
    S2, O3

Oakley, Hampshire S4
Oldham, Greater Manchester E6
Orpington, Kent S9
Overton, Hampshire S2
Oxford, Oxfordshire S2, S5, O1

Paignton, Devon O8
Pembroke, Wales O2
Penarth, Wales E5, O4
Penrith, Cumbria S3
Penhurst, Kent O3, O9
Peterborough, Cambridgeshire
    S1
Peterlee, Durham S2
Pewsey, Wiltshire S2
Pinner, Greater London O6
Plumstead, Greater London S15,
    E7
Plymouth, Devon S5, O2, O4,
    O9
Porthtowan, Cornwall S3
Porthywaen, Shropshire S2
Preston, Lancashire E2, O1
Pudsey, West Yorkshire S6, O1

Quainton, Buckinghamshire O2

Radlett, Hertfordshire S9
Rayne, Essex S7
Reading, Berkshire O1
Redbridge, Essex E1
Rhydyfelin, Wales S8
Rhos-on-Sea, Wales O1
Ripon, North Yorkshire O3
Rochdale, Lancashire S7
Roehampton, Greater London S4
Romsey, Hampshire S3
Rossendale, Lancashire S3, S11,
    O3
Rotherham, South Yorkshire S2
Rothley, Leicestershire S1
Rutland, Leicestershire S2

St Albans, Hertfordshire E1
St Helens, Merseyside S2
Saltburn, Cleveland S3
Salford, Greater Manchester S3
Salisbury, Wiltshire S3, O5
Sawston, Cambridgeshire S2
Saxmundham, Suffolk S2, E2
Scarborough, North Yorkshire
    S4, E1, O5
Selhurst Park, Greater London
    O14
Sevenoaks, Kent E6, S6
Sheffield, South Yorkshire S1,
    S4, S6, S7, E3, O2
Shepshed, Leicestershire S3,
    O1
Sheringham, Norfolk S4
Shildon, Durham S3, O1
Shipley, West Yorkshire S7
Shirley, Surrey S3
Skelmersdale, Lancashire O4
Slough, Berkshire E1

Smethwick, West Midlands E7
Solihull, West Midlands E9
Southall, Greater London E10
Southampton, Hampshire S9, E2
Southbourne, Dorset O2
Southport, Merseyside S3
Sproughton, Suffolk S3
Stafford, Staffordshire S2, O1
Standish, Greater Manchester S2
Stanmore, Greater London E12
Stanton, Derbyshire O1
Stevenage, Hertfordshire S4
Stockport, Cheshire O4, S3
Stockton-on-Tees, Cleveland S1,
    S4
Stogumber, Somerset S3
Stoke Newington, Greater
    London E11
Stoke-on-Trent, Staffordshire S3
Stony Stratford,
    Buckinghamshire S3
Stourbridge, West Midlands S6,
    E5
Stowmarket, Suffolk S5
Sunderland, Tyne and Wear S1
Surbiton, Surrey S1, O1
Sutton-in-Ashfield,
    Nottinghamshire O3
Sutton Coldfield, West Midlands
    S4
Swacetown, Derbyshire S3
Swadlincote, Derbyshire S8
Swaffham, Norfolk S3
Swansea, Wales O5
Swanwick, Derbyshire S2, S4, S8
Swindon, Wiltshire S4, S5
Syderstone, Norfolk S9

Taunton, Somerset S2, O2
Thetford, Norfolk S6
Thorpe-le-Soken, Essex S11
Tibshelf, Derbyshire S1
Tinsley, South Yorkshire E2
Torbay, Devon O1
Tottington, Lancashire S4
Towcester, Northamptonshire S3,
    S5
Trawden, Lancashire S2
Tring, Hertfordshire S11
Trowbridge, Wiltshire S1
Truro, Cornwall S1

Wadebridge, Cornwall S8
Wakefield, West Midlands O3
Wallasey, Merseyside O1
Wallsend, Tyne and Wear E1
Waltham Forest, Greater London
    S10
Ware, Hertfordshire S5
Warminster, Wiltshire O2
Warrington, Cheshire O5
Warwick, Warwickshire S1, S5,
    O1, O3
Watford, Hertfordshire S12, E2
Welling, Kent O1

Wellingborough,
   Northamptonshire O2
Wembley, Greater London E8, E9
West Bromwich, West Midlands
   S9, E2, O1
Westcott, Buckinghamshire O4
West Norwood, Greater London
   E2
Weston Favell, Northamptonshire
   O1
Whitstable, Kent O7
Widnes, Cheshire S7
Wigan, Greater Manchester S1
Wimborne, Dorset S3, S5
Wilmington, Kent S8, O9
Winchester, Hampshire O1
Wingfield, Derbyshire S5
Witchford, Cambridgeshire O2
Wolverhampton, West Midlands
   E6, E10
Worthing, West Sussex S2
Wraysbury, Berkshire S1
Wrexham, Wales S3, E1

Yarmouth, Norfolk S1
Yeovil, Somerset O1
York, North Yorkshire O1, O6
Ystrad Mynach, Wales S7